Whose School is it Anyway?

Educational Change and Development Series

Series Editors: Andy Hargreaves, Ontario Institute for Studies in Education, Canada and
Ivor F Goodson, Warner Graduate School, University of Rochester, USA and Centre for Applied Research in Education, University of East Anglia, Norwich, UK

Whose School is it Anyway?

Kathryn A. Riley

FALMER PRESS
Taylor & Francis Group

UK   Falmer Press, 1 Gunpowder Square, London, EC4A 3DE
USA   Falmer Press, Taylor & Francis Inc., 1900 Frost Road, Suite 101,
Bristol, PA 19007

First published in 1998

A catalogue record for this book is available from the British Library

ISBN 0 7507 07135 cased
ISBN 0 7507 06716 paper

Library of Congress Cataloging-in-Publication Data are available on request

Jacket design by Caroline Archer

Typeset in 11/13pt Garamond by
Graphicraft Typesetters Ltd., Hong Kong

Printed in Great Britain by Biddles Ltd., Guildford and King's Lynn on paper which has a specified pH value on final paper manufacture of not less than 7.5 and is therefore 'acid free'.

Contents

Preface and Acknowledgments

If one is to believe in education at all, one must believe that something worth doing can be done.
And if one is to believe in anything, one must believe in education . . .
The moral for the educator is to be more ambitious.
F.R. Leavis and Denys Thompson (1934, p. 4)

The Labour Government of 1997 has an historic opportunity to lay the foundations of a new national education consensus, similar to that which prevailed for some thirty years after the Second World War. This book examines why that post-war consensus broke down in the mid-1970s, and how in the 1980s, the Thatcherite revolution transformed the educational landscape. It draws on a wide range of educational research from around the world to examine questions which teachers and educational reformers are struggling with in many countries besides the UK. Both historical and contemporary events are used to reflect on some of the possible elements of the new educational dispensation between central and local government, teachers, governors, parents and pupils. Some of the questions and events which I explore are, inevitably, those which have interested me through my journey in education as a teacher, elected local councillor, local government officer, governor, parent and most recently as an academic researcher.

The book is not a polemic, nor is it prescriptive. But it poses many of the questions and some of my answers to the issues of the day. It represents a distillation of my work over recent years — work that has been influenced by many people. There are those who I interviewed for the book (see Appendix I). Conducting those interviews was a delight and it gave me the opportunity to venture into unusual places — my thanks to the interviewees, particularly Anne Page, for the extensive and rich source material, and Fred Jarvis and Peter Newsam for pointing me in the direction of a number of gems.

I would also like to thank my research colleagues at the Centre for Educational Management at Roehampton, David Rowles and Jim Docking, with support from Ian Monk, and colleagues from Scotland, Denmark and Australia who were part of the research team on school leadership (see Chapter 8). Particular thanks go to Pat Mahony and John MacBeath. My work has also been influenced not just by the research I have undertaken but by the experiences and challenges of many of those teachers, headteachers, governors, pupils, LEA officers and politicians who have taken part in the various projects. Thanks to them.

There are those who have contributed to my thinking over the years and who also commented on this book. I would particularly like to thank here Alan Ruby and Gerald Grace. I would also like to mention two friends who died recently, Desmond Nuttall and Kieron Walsh. Both in their different ways contributed to my thinking and development, as have Margaret Sandra, Judy White, Tanya Arroba and Vivien Lowndes. I would like to thank members of the Education Reform Group, educationalists who always offer challenging thinking on new developments in education, and those colleagues who attended the 1997 conference on teachers and professionalism (see Chapter 9).

Finally, I would also like thank my family — near and far — who include my toughest critics and greatest supporters. My daughter Jo is a constant reminder of the spirited questioning of young people. My mother, Agnes Riley, was a teacher and although she died in 1988, she remains a strong influence on me. She exemplified the commitment and passion for teaching which today is so easily forgotten, and so rarely valued as the mainspring of all educational success.

Kathryn Riley
January 1998

Part I

Constructing the Reform Agenda

Chapter 1

Your School or Mine?

The central point of the dispute is: To whom does the school belong? To the family, to the community, to the church, or to the State? All these are interested in the school. The problem is: Can their various interests be united by a just consideration of their various rights and duties? (Professor W. Rein, University of Jena, Cambridge lecture, 1909, Quoted in W.O. Lester Smith, 1946, p. 7)

In 1997, the newly elected Labour Government launched a White Paper on Education entitled, *Excellence in Schools* which resulted in the following newspaper headline: *Government to have its hand in every school* (Independent 1997a). The idea that education should be a national concern has been with us for well over a century. The issue today, particularly following a change of government after 18 years of Conservative administrations, is how far those concerns should extend.

This book is about schools: who rules them, and who uses them. Schools reflect the aspirations of communities, both for individuals within that community and for the community as a whole. What those aspirations are and how far they are shared by all those who make up that education community are questions at the heart of our conundrum: 'whose school is it anyway?'

I want to question whether we have got the balance of powers and responsibilities right in relation to schools. Has the pendulum swung too far in the direction of government, or not far enough? Should greater powers be given to governors, students, parents? Have we got the decision-making configuration we need? Should there be some settlement — rather than an uneasy truce — between central and local government? I also want to examine how those involved in school governance, central and local government, headteachers and governors, can each contribute to providing a climate of challenge and inquiry. A climate in which teachers take responsibility for their own professional development and are given the opportunities to think, reflect and take action, and in which students are given the tools, the knowledge base and the confidence to think for themselves.

The questions which I want to explore are not unique to the UK and many of them will be shared by those involved in education reform in other countries. The UK's answers to those questions, however, will be of particular interest to others because for a number of years, education reformers have looked to developments in the UK, either as models to be emulated, or ones to be avoided. I hope the book will shed new light on the education reforms of the UK and on the process of educational reform in general.

Tyndale and Ruskin

The book begins by stepping back into the history of two events in the 1970s: the conflict at the William Tyndale Junior School in Islington, and Prime Minister James Callaghan's Ruskin speech. William Tyndale was a sixteenth century religious reformer and the person responsible for translating the Bible into English — an initiative in popular education which led to wide-spread controversy and his eventual execution. He was strangled and burned at the stake in 1536. The London school named after him, William Tyndale Junior School, became a cause celebre in 1975.

William Tyndale School proved to be as controversial as its patron. It influenced national thinking about education and gave succour to those who thought that something was radically wrong with schools. Both political ideology and educational philosophy went on trial at Tyndale. To many, Tyndale was the failing school in which left-wing motivated teachers put ideology before classroom practice and created a climate of student underachievement. To others, it was the school in which dedicated left-wing teachers had tried to offer working-class children real choices and a broad educational experience, and had been pilloried by the press for their pains. William Tyndale became national press headlines just as the new Prime Minister of the day, James Callaghan, was preparing a major speech on education — his Ruskin speech. The press painted a picture of Tyndale as a school which was out of control, teachers who had become too powerful, and a local authority which had failed in its responsibilities.

The newspaper headlines for James Callaghan's Ruskin speech were not quite as dramatic, or sustained, as the coverage of William Tyndale. Nevertheless, Ruskin caused significant waves, particularly in the education press. Callaghan questioned both the costs and outcomes of state education and challenged what he saw as teacher domination of schools and the curriculum. The speech was seen by some pundits of the day as inappropriate interference by a Prime Minister who knew nothing about education: by others, as a breath of fresh air in the closed world of education.

Events at Tyndale undoubtedly placed on the national agenda issues to do with the professional autonomy of teachers and headteachers, the control of schools, and who had the right to 'intervene' if things went wrong. Tyndale went badly adrift because of the fragmentation of responsibilities between governors, teachers, the local authority and, to some extent, parents. Tyndale and Ruskin combined to call into question the autonomy of teachers; the authority of headteachers; and the role of parents, the local authority and national government. The core purposes and outcomes of education became national issues in ways that were new to education.

The explorations into events at Tyndale and into the genesis of the Ruskin speech which are presented in this book are far from being mere historical musings. They have a contemporary resonance and through looking at events at William Tyndale, the question 'who rules our schools?' — is it teachers, the headteacher, governors, pupils, parents, politicians, or local officials? — is starkly posed. A further reason for embarking on this historical exploration was curiosity. I began my teaching career in the 1970s. Both Tyndale and Ruskin are part of the backcloth which shaped my experience of teaching in London in the 1970s and 1980s, and my journey through education ever since. I attended meetings at which Tyndale school was hotly debated and I have a vivid recollection of Brian Haddow (one of the key figures in events at Tyndale) giving his account of events at one of those meetings. Whilst Callaghan's Ruskin speech did not impinge on my daily experience as a London teacher in quite the same way, nevertheless, it struck a discordant note. As a consequence, I have always wanted to explore whether it really was a 'watershed' in education as many pundits have claimed.

It has been fascinating to look at both events, if not afresh, in the context of a new political era ushered in by the election of a Labour Government. I have tried to use the events of the 1970s to illustrate the shifting sands of school governance: the changing powers, relationships and responsibilities of those involved in education at national, intermediary and school levels. The distance of time does not lend enchantment but gives us the opportunity to reflect on events with a fresh eye and to understand both where things have changed, and where they have remained the same. In revisiting both Tyndale and Ruskin and examining their legacies, I have drawn on contemporary accounts, as well as carrying out a number of interviews with key individuals who were involved in those events (see Appendix I). Their stories are recast in the light of the current debates in education.

An essential element of this book has also been about trying to gain some understanding of what has influenced some of the key actors who helped shape the policy agenda at a particular moment in time. What were the personal experiences, beliefs and prejudices which influenced their thinking, and what were the particular political and historical configurations and events which combined to shape the policy agenda? What, for example, drove events at Tyndale to their dramatic conclusion? What influenced the Ruskin speech? To what extent were the events at William Tyndale and Ruskin connected? Did Callaghan get it right? Did the Ruskin speech pave the way for the Conservative reform agenda? To what extent did sheer chance or sound judgment play their parts?

Both Tyndale and Ruskin illustrate the ways in which our thinking about schools is shaped by particular events and how those events in their turn influence policy. Policy is not inert and, indeed, the policy process is a constantly moving loop: an organic activity shaped by ideologies, idiosyncrasies, power struggles, structural alliances and personalities. Policy is constantly reinterpreted in the light of high profile events, media interpretation of these events, organizational and institutional concerns, and in the light of practice. Looking to the future, policy will be reshaped by new ideologies. New power struggles and structural alliances will emerge and different personalities with their own idiosyncrasies, prejudices and goals will each play their part. It is impossible to predict quite what will happen, or how particular configurations will combine to ignite the education flame, all of which makes the 'business' of tracking policy a fascinating one.

School Governance

Events at Tyndale cause us to examine the powers and responsibilities of all those involved in school governance. But they also enable us to focus on the role of headteachers and how they contribute to the climate of success, or failure, in a school. I want to examine what it means to be an effective school leader and to explore whether we have the kinds of leaders and the kinds of leadership that we need for the twenty-first century, not only in schools but also in local education authorities.

Over recent years, the conditions of and demands on headteachers, college principals and directors of education have changed beyond recognition. I want to suggest, however, that there is no one package for leadership of the education service, no one model to be learned and applied in unrefined forms for all schools, colleges, or local education authorities. Nor is leadership something that is carried out by one brave charismatic person leading unwilling troops into battle. The 'heroic' model of leadership has some attractions but also many weaknesses. Good leadership is not only shared amongst senior staff, but in a vibrant school which is a professional community, other staff will also take on important leadership roles, and pupils will also feel that they are part of a school community, not inmates in an institution.

In looking at school governance I want to look at our school system from a number of vantage points: from the view point of the schools themselves (headteachers, staff, pupils and governors); from the view point of parents and the wider school community; and from the view point of local and central governments. Schools do not exist in a vacuum. They are at the very heart of our education system and should be part of a coherent whole. However, changes over recent years have increasingly driven schools to operate in isolation from one another.

We have witnessed the introduction of market forces into education — what has come to be described as the 'marketization' of education. Parents have been encouraged to be active 'consumers' and to exercise their 'rights'. Competition has been created as a way of providing greater diversity and choice. A certain amount of deregulation has been introduced in areas such as school admissions. But choice has its limitations. Parents exercise their preference for a school, but where there is competition for places, schools chose the pupils. While market forces have increased the awareness of schools about performance and about accountability, they have also increased social selection and exclusion, creating winners and losers. These issues add a particular edge to the question: 'whose school is it anyway?'

As we move towards the twenty-first century, politicians everywhere will need to take stock and examine the restructuring of education which has taken place over recent years. Governments today face many challenges in education. They need to look carefully at the impact of the structural reforms which have been a major preoccupation over recent years, and question how far those reforms have created radical changes in what actually goes on in classrooms between teacher and pupil, and pupil and pupil. The curriculum has been adjusted, our notions of professionalism have also been adjusted, but the dominating mode of instruction — an adult who will make children learn — largely remains the same (Ruby, 1995).

The impact of restructuring In the UK has been mixed. Some aspects of the reforms have added to the strengths of our system, others have eaten away at the foundations and have left us with a number of contradictions and dilemmas:

- Local management of schools has enabled headteachers to take responsibility for administrative decisions in their schools; but at the expense of time spent with pupils;
- The introduction of the National Curriculum has forced teachers to have more defined work programmes; but at the expense of personal judgment and imagination;
- The introduction of the national inspection system has called to account a number of schools which were simply not delivering what children deserved; but has diverted resources from school improvement and led to fear and anger amongst good teachers as well as bad.

What is immediately clear, is that national governments need to reconsider their role in the complex educational process. Schools do not belong just to the government of the day. National government must set the lead but will only really be successful in its objectives where it works in tandem with its partners and creates new forms of partnership. In a fast moving and complex society, the role of national government must be increasingly to promote learning, rather than to direct systems. Direction will simply not work. A 'command and surveillance' culture such as that inherited by the 1997 Labour Government will stifle the creativity and flexibility required for the future. The challenge is to move back from maintenance and control towards influence and development, while maintaining clear accountability mechanisms. Politicians will need to ask themselves such critical questions as:

- How can we enthuse and inspire teachers?
- Have we got the balance of power and decision-making right in the system?
- Is the education market-place working? (And if so, to whose benefit?)
- What intermediary levels of government do we need to support us in our national objectives and to reflect local priorities?
- In what ways must teaching and learning be recast to meet the challenges for the twenty-first century?

Chapter 2

The End of an Era

> The school sets out deliberately to devise the right environment for children, to allow then to be themselves and to develop in the way and at the pace appropriate for them. It tries to equalise opportunities and to compensate for handicaps. It lays special stress on individual discovery, on first hand experience and on opportunities for creative work. It insists that knowledge does not fall into neatly separate compartments and that work and play are not opposite but complementary. Plowden (1967, para. 505)

The 1960s and early 1970s were periods of rapid social and cultural change, shaped by post-war forces and by new radical forces. Tyndale and Ruskin signalled that the post-war consensus about education had come to an end. The 1944 Education Act, implemented in the first flush of post-war optimism, had established the framework for that consensus and the boundaries of professional and political control of education which lasted for some two decades. The configuration was one in which national government set a broad agenda and provided distant oversight of the school system. Local authorities interpreted the national agenda and were responsible for the delivery of education, although there were limited ways in which they were called to account publicly for outcomes. Teachers largely determined curriculum and pedagogy, although some boundaries were set by the examination bodies and by local authorities through the allocation of resources and the establishment of local priorities.

The 1944 Act also brought about the creation of the tripartite system of grammar, technical and secondary modern schools for 11 year olds. The secondary schools, although of 'diversified types', were intended to be of equal standing. Children were to be educated to 'their age, aptitude and ability,' but the economic depression of the late 1950s and drastic cuts in public expenditure, resulted in reductions in investment in technical education (Peers, 1963) and the tripartite system became, in effect, a bipartite system of grammar and secondary modern schools in many areas of the country. Children who passed the 'eleven-plus' went to grammar school, those who 'failed', to a secondary modern school.

By the 1960s, the selective system overall had come under scrutiny. Critics argued that selection at 11, and early streaming in primary schools had reinforced social class inequality and created a 'wastage' of ability in those working-class children who were rejected by the system (Vernon, 1957; Floud, 1961). Advocates of the comprehensive school argued (in terms which echoed many of the sentiments of segregation and exclusion which were part of the US Civil Rights' agenda at the time) that comprehensives would help create cohesiveness, social harmony and social justice in society (Benn and Chitty, 1996). Selection merely reflected social class, rather than ability.

The Comprehensive Seesaw

Comprehensive education emerged on the national political agenda following Harold Wilson's Labour election success in 1964. The Wilson Government, elected with a majority of four, promised to put an end to 'Thirteen Wasted Tory Years' by harnessing the 'White Heat of the Technological Revolution'. In *the Future of Socialism,* Tony Crosland had put forward his thinking about the nature of society (Crosland, 1956). Egalitarianism was to be at the centre of Labour policy and a move away from selection at age 11 towards comprehensive education was an essential element in the drive towards an egalitarian society. When Tony Crosland took the helm in education, the Labour Government gave a strong steer towards comprehensive education.

In 1965, 8.5 per cent of the secondary school population were in comprehensive schools (Rubinstein and Simon, 1973, p. 109). Tony Crosland, in a now famous Circular 10/65, 'requested' local authorities to put forward plans for comprehensive education rather than 'required' them to take action, as some supporters of comprehensive education had advocated. The final wording of the Circular was a personal decision on the part of Crosland himself and reflected his determination to try and build up a consensus on the matter (Kogan, 1971, p. 189). Whether the Labour Government should have been tougher in its plan to introduce comprehensive education has remained an issue for dispute (Benn and Chitty, 1996). However, the Crosland strategy undoubtedly provoked considerable debate about comprehensive education:

A remarkable benefit accrued from the loose rein with which Mr Crosland handled the matter. It sparked off a tremendous democratic debate on our schools and what was to be done about them, throughout the length and breadth of England. Never before can there have been so many public meetings, so many working parties, so many inches of correspondence in columns in the local and national press devoted to education . . . It has brought ordinary parents inside the school doors mentally, and often physically, for the first time, instead of leaving them shunned on the outside. (Pedley, 1963, p. 57)

By the following year 1966, however, the Labour Government had moved into a tougher mode and had begun to apply financial leverage to try and encourage local authorities to put forward plans for comprehensive reorganization. Government Circular 10/66 made it clear that resources for secondary school building would not be made available to local authorities, unless their buildings proposals contributed to comprehensive reorganization. Despite this push, central government's influence on local authority decisions remained weak and in 1967 and 1968, as a result of Conservative victories in local authority elections, a number of comprehensive reorganization plans were withdrawn by local education authorities. In 1970, the Labour Government introduced a Bill aimed at giving the government powers to introduce comprehensive education but the Bill failed and soon after, a Conservative Government was elected.

The new Secretary of State for Education, Margaret Thatcher, introduced her own Circular 10/70 which cancelled Tony Crosland's previous advice and told local authorities that they could keep grammar schools. But by 1970, the move towards comprehensive reorganization had achieved a momentum of its own, embraced by a number of Conservative, as well as Labour local authorities. Ironically, during Mrs Thatcher's time as Secretary of State, more grammar schools were closed, and more comprehensive schools created, than at any other time, before or since (Timmins, 1995).

Despite the heated debate about comprehensive or selective education, the framework established by the 1944 Education Act, which had emphasized local autonomy and professional responsibility for the delivery of services, remained largely intact through both the Conservative and Labour administrations of the 1960s and early 1970s. How schools were to be managed, or judged for their performance, were not issues of central concern to government. It was still teachers who largely determined school practice and how objectives should be achieved within schools. Throughout the 1960s, there remained an anticipation that education opportunities would continue to grow and that schools could provide those opportunities. Such assumptions were coupled with a belief that education could help tackle social disadvantage, aided by a broad intellectual, largely progressive, consensus about schools which found expression in the Plowden Report.

Progressive Education and the Plowden Report

The Plowden Committee had been set up by the Wilson Government to look at primary education and the transition to secondary education. Writing in the Introduction to the report, Tony Crosland, as Secretary of State for Education, expressed the hope that Plowden would 'enable decisions to be reached on a more informed basis by those who are charged with securing the best development of English education' (Plowden, 1967, Introduction).

The Report offered a clear articulation of the objectives of primary education and the role that schools could play in tackling social disadvantage. Maurice Kogan (who was secretary to the Committee) recalled, in an interview with me in 1996, the Committee's approach, and the climate of the times:

> The Committee took a substantial amount of evidence about what was happening in junior schools[1]. Committee members also made a number of visits, for example, to Russia and were horrified at the rigidity of the system. At the time, there was a broad intellectual consensus about education and a view that schools themselves had the ability to deliver what was necessary. There was, however, a certain inertia about quality issues in schools. Everybody signed up for the descant of progressive education. There were also strong views about social engineering.

The principles and practice of primary education outlined in Plowden were drawn up in the philosophical traditions of Susan Issacs, Jerome Bruner and Jean Piaget, amongst others. Behaviourist interpretations of learning, associated with psychologists such as Pavlov or Skinner, were largely rejected. Learning was seen as a 'continuous process of interaction between the learner and his environment' (Plowden, paras. 519–20). Children were deemed to be intrinsically interested in learning (ibid. para. 532): a view strongly at odds with that of the Chief Inspector of Schools in 1997, Chris Woodhead (Woodhead, 1997). Schools transmitted important values about society, which Plowden described in the following terms:

> A school is not merely a teaching shop, it must transmit values and attitudes. It is a community in which children learn to live first and foremost as children and not as future adults. In family life, children learn to live with people of all ages . . . A child brought up in such an atmosphere at all stages of 'his' education has some hope of becoming a balanced and mature adult and of being able to live in, to contribute to, and to look critically at the society of which he forms a part. (ibid. para. 505)

As well as providing a clear philosophy, Plowden outlined the practical implications of progressive education in some detail. Flexibility was the key and both the primary school timetable and the curriculum needed that flexibility in order to 'make good use of the interest and curiosity of children' (ibid, para. 540). Schools were encouraged to draw on the local environment; to maximize learning and create opportunities for children to extend their thinking through project work, group work, individualized, as well as class activities. The pursuit of curiosity, creativity and inquiry came to be accepted as some of the basic tenets of progressive education.

Plowden encouraged teachers to place a strong reliance on the capacity of children to learn for themselves, but the authors also argued for a clear framework for learning. Boundaries were to be set. 'From the start' said the authors, 'there must be teaching as well as learning'. Children were not 'free' to develop interests or skills of which they had no knowledge: an issue which staff at Tyndale were later to dispute. Schools needed to enable children to be adaptable, so that they could adjust to a changing environment.

> (Children) will need to be capable of *being taught*, and of *learning* the new skills called for by the changing economic scene . . . and understand that in a democratic society each individual has obligations to the community, as well as rights within it. (ibid. para. 496)

Children needed guidance from their teachers (ibid. para. 754). Pupils were not to be given free choice (ibid. para. 530). According to Plowden, the word discovery had been 'loosely interpreted and had often been misunderstood' and critics of progressive education had been right to suggest that trivial ideas and inefficient methods could also be 'discovered'. A balance needed to be struck which recognized that time constraints did not allow children to find their way by discovery to all that they have to learn (ibid. para. 549). Creativity and curiosity were not, in Plowden's view, in opposition to other more traditional education goals but were complementary to them. 'Neatness, accuracy, care and perseverance and the sheer knowledge' were essential parts of education and were 'genuine virtues' which education needed to foster (ibid. para. 506). Progressive teaching methods such as team-teaching were to be encouraged and streaming, particularly early streaming, was discouraged.

For those who have not experienced the impact of early streaming in primary schools, let me add here a personal recollection. When I was six, I lost all my friends at school. Or so it seemed to me. It was many years later before I came to understand what had happened. My birthday is in July which means that I started school in the Easter just before I was five. For that first term, I was taught with 24 other summer born children and because the school was so overcrowded, our classroom was the school hall. I know about the number and the hall because some years later I met my first teacher who reminded me of these details. The school had two other classes of 5 year olds who had joined the school in the term in which their fifth birthday took place. After a term we 'summer born' children joined those classes. When I was six, my fate was sealed. The school divided all the 6 year olds into three classes by 'ability'. At the time this decision was made, children such as myself had only been in the school four terms. Our performance was 'measured' against that of children who had been in the school for either five, or six terms. I was the only 'four-termer' to make it to the 'A' stream. It was only children in the 'A' stream who stood any real chance of passing the 'Eleven Plus' and going to grammar school. I remember being told how well I had done to go into the 'A' stream but I also remember the sense of bewilderment.

Plowden's arguments about early streaming recognized the real problems associated with dividing children up by 'ability' at such an early age. Plowden also argued that there had been too much class instruction and that a greater *balance* needed to be achieved between class teaching, individualized learning and group work (ibid. para. 537). Given current debates about progressive versus traditional education, it is important to reflect on this issue of balance.

Plowden did, however, oppose attainment standards on the grounds that, 'Any set of standards would seriously limit the bright child and be impossibly high for the dull' (ibid. para. 551). It argued instead for recurring national surveys on pupil attainment and regular feedback to primary schools from secondary schools, on the comparative performance of children from different primary schools (ibid. para. 554). In order to ensure that children were making progress, monitoring and careful record keeping were essential (ibid. para. 279): again something which as Chapter 3 suggests, was largely ignored at Tyndale.

Plowden was far from being an anarchist's charter, as some on both sides of the dispute at Tyndale later interpreted it. In some schools, it did became an excuse for sloppy practices. As one interviewee for this book explained to me, 'Projects used to make me weep. There was a lot of good heartedness but little rigour'. But the same interviewee also went on to argue that Plowden had served to challenge many unaccepted practices in primary education and to bring parents into the equation. Until Plowden, many schools still had notices which said,

'No parents beyond this point'. Plowden emphasized parental participation and home-school partnerships and argued that parents should be allowed to choose their child's primary school whenever this was possible.

It is difficult to disentangle the extent to which Plowden reflected what was happening in primary school, or promoted a shift towards progressive education: no doubt it was a mixture of both. What is clear is that the Plowden agenda was a common agenda for many in education — shared by teachers, as well as the politicians of the day. In 1972, as Secretary of State for Education, Margaret Thatcher presided over an expansionist education budget which supported many of the priorities set by Plowden, particularly in relation to early years. Her White Paper, 'Education a Framework for Expansion', put forward a range of plans, including raising of the school-leaving age and extensive expansion of nursery education which, if implemented, would have brought about a rise in education spending of some 50 per cent over a decade (Timmins, 1995, p. 301). Margaret Thatcher also embraced one of the central tenets of Plowden: the need to tackle social disadvantage. As she recalls in her biography:

> You found that by the time children came to school at the age of five, a lot of them were already behind . . . Of course the State can never take the place of good parents . . . but it can help redress the balance. (Gardiner, 1975, p. 111)

The Plowden Report posed some of the questions which educationalists are still grappling with today.

- Is there a genuine conflict between education based on children as they are, and education thought of primarily as a preparation for the future?
- Has 'finding out' proved to be better than 'being told'?
- How can headteachers and and class teachers arrange the internal work of each school and class to meet the different needs of the highly gifted boys and girls, of slow learning pupils, and of all the infinite varieties of talent and interest that lie between? (ibid. para. 6)

Both critics of the day and recent critics have tended to present an over-simplified view of the arguments presented in the Plowden Report. In the 1990s, there have been calls to suggest that 'Plowdenism' retains a stranglehold on our education system, generating relativist views about pupil performance, rather than belief in absolute standards of achievement to be expected from all pupils. Melanie Phillips, for example, has argued that many contemporary problems in education can be traced back to Plowden, 'the bible of of child-centred education' (Phillips, 1996, p. 57). Critics of progressive education have implied wrongly that Plowden advocated one approach to teaching and learning. The issue, as we shall see in Chapter 3 is not what Plowden advocated but how people have chosen to interpret it. Recent debates have also centred on the extent to which teachers need to be trained to teach pupils, or to teach subjects (see, for example, Phillips, 1996; Guardian, 1997a). As I will suggest later, this is as false and unnecessarily polarized a debate in the 1990s, as it was in the 1960s.

Education in Transition

Gradually the liberal and optimistic mood of the times which characterized Plowden began to change. A general anxiety about the state of society had begun to emerge in the late 1960s and early 1970s. There was a questioning of old certainties and a challenge to the established order, symbolized by the student revolts and opposition to the Vietnam War. There was a growing unease about the nature of society and its capacity to fulfil all that it had appeared to promise to the post-war generation. In 1975, Tony Crosland put a break on local government spending and announced that 'the party was over' (Timmins, 1995, p. 313). Unemployment had began to rise and despite the 'Barber' boom in 1970–1972, the 1970s was also marked by a decline in economic growth and a general curb on prosperity.

The 1970s did, however, also witness a rapid expansion of higher education which opened opportunities to a broader section of the community and served to raise aspirations, but there were growing concerns about whether those aspirations could be realized. Expansionist and progressive thinking about education was gradually challenged and there was also an emerging belief that schools could no longer provide all the opportunities that were needed. Maurice Kogan has described these changes and the growing disillusionment with education, in the following terms:

> Education is a gigantic case study of how increased social and individual activity and commitment — more expenditure, more building, more people, and more political support — do not necessarily lead

to satisfaction and success . . . By the end of 1977 only the daring or the self-interested were able to call for more educational growth as a certain way to economic salvation. (Kogan, 1978, pp. 25–41)

Throughout the 1970s, the debate about selective or comprehensive education also continued, with growing concerns from one camp about secondary modern schools, and from the other about the demise of grammar schools. Some of the disillusion about education could be seen in the growing right-wing critique of state education which had first emerged in the late 1960s and early 1970s in what came to be known as 'The Black Papers'. The first of these papers (which were in many ways a disparate set of essays on education) was published in 1969 by academics Brian Cox and Tony Dyson, who edited a small but influential journal called the 'Critical Survey'. The Paper emerged in the wake of student unrest in the USA, France and the UK — Brian Cox had spent some time at the University of California Berkeley at the height of the student protests and the Paper criticized the student revolts. James Callaghan was another person to be influenced by the student unrest, as is discussed in Chapter 5. In 1968, he was the British Home Secretary when student protests hit the streets of London and the university campuses.

The first Black Paper also attacked comprehensive education and progressive teaching methods. It blamed the apparent destruction of authority in universities and secondary schools on progressive education (Cox and Dyson, 1971). The label 'Black Paper' appears to have emerged initially as a joke by Tony Dyson who contrasted Black Paperite comments about the 'real' state of education with government views expressed in a variety of 'White Papers' (official discussion documents which usually pave the way for legislation). The term gained wider currency in 1969 when, in a speech to the National Union of Teachers, Ted Short (who was Secretary of State for Education at that time) condemned the publication of the Paper, and particularly the attack on comprehensive education as, 'one of the blackest days for education in the past 100 years' (Short, quoted in Timmins, 1995, p. 273). Many others shared this view[2]. Ted Short's lambasting attracted press interest and brought the first Black Paper to the attention of a wider audience, including Rhodes Boyson who was to became a central figure in the progressive/traditionalist educational battle. At the time of the publication, he was headteacher of Highbury Grove Boys School in Islington, close to William Tyndale School. He was later to edit two of the Black Papers and become a Conservative MP and junior Education Minister, before finally losing his seat in the 1997 election. Rhodes Boyson also played a small but significant role in events at William Tyndale school, as is discussed in Chapter 3.

Over a period of years, the five Black Papers offered a growing critique of state education and attracted considerable press interest. It was purported that requiring grammar schools to accept pupils of all abilities had been an attack on excellence. The introduction of comprehensive education had brought about a lowering of standards. Greater consumer choice and accountability in education, coupled with greater control of the education professional, would bring about an increase in standards (Ranson and Thomas, 1989; Riley, 1992). The Black Papers became part of a political attack on state education. But concerns about teaching methods had surfaced in 1975 in an exploratory study which later came to be seen as a seminal work, *Education and Social Control* (Sharp and Green with Lewis, 1975).

Rachel Sharp and Anthony Green proffered a major critique of progressive methods in primary education which challenged the consensus of the day. They argued that lack of structure had damaged opportunities for working-class children. Child-centred methodology was not clearly articulated by staff and there were often conflicting expectations about what was achievable. Child-centred approaches — which had been seen as radical alternatives to formal, authoritarian and elitist approaches to education — had became in reality individualistic and voluntarist approaches which were a modern form of conservatism: a new form of social control. The implication of the adoption of such approaches was that:

> Children tended to be given wide discretion to choose between many activities, and in so far as they appeared to choose things, i.e. satisfied the condition of 'busyness' the child-centred approach was assumed to be in operation. (ibid. p. 216)

Education and Social Control did not spring from the same ideological stable as the Black Papers. The questions which it raised matched the concerns of a number of influential figures including members of the Central Policy Review staff at Number 10 (such as Tessa Blackstone) who advised the Prime Minister of the day, Jim Callaghan (see Chapter 5).

It was the Black Papers, however, which began to dominate the political stage. Many of the ideas from the Papers surfaced in the writings of a number of the right-wing 'Think Tanks' which strongly influenced Conservative thinking in education in the 1980s (see Knight, 1990). Egalitarianism was a primary target and the 'Black Paperites' challenged the equity and social justice arguments which had held political sway in the 1960s and early 1970s. The 1977 Black Paper which Rhodes Boyson co-edited with Brian Cox, for example, gave prominence to the following quotation:

> Egalitarianism encourages the lazy and the passive at the expense of the dedicated and the diligent. Dubcek, Czechoslovak Communist Manifesto, 1968 (Quoted in Cox and Boyson, 1977, p. 55)

The influential Centre for Policy Studies was later to publish a pamphlet on a similar theme entitled *End Egalitarian Delusion* (CPS, 1991), a favourite theme of David Willetts, past director of the CPS, ex-Conservative Minister and, since June 1997, a Shadow Conservative Minister of Education. In his own book, David Willetts was to argue that equality and egalitarianism were unfortunate but seductive remnants of socialism which had to be eradicated:

> There is one key idea, seductive and with a strong emotional appeal which cannot be absorbed into Conservative thought: egalitarianism. (Willetts, 1992, p. 109)

Both Tyndale and Ruskin have, therefore, to be viewed in the context of what was to become the battle ground for ideas which were to shape the foundations of the educational reforms of the 1980s and 1990s. I describe this as a battle ground because views became increasingly polarized. There was the battle between egalitarianism and meritocracy which focused on selection. There was the battle between progressive and traditional teaching methods. Plowden came to epitomize progressive teaching and the Black Paperites increasingly saw themselves as the defenders of standards, protectors of the grammar school. There was the battle about the nature of schooling itself: was the role of schools to counter past inequalities, or create avenues for individuals to find the fast track to the top?

The battle for ideas was played out at many levels: in the Black Papers and the many articles and books which challenged, or supported that analysis; in the 'Think Tanks' and Policy Forums; and in the plans to introduce comprehensive schools, or 'save' grammar schools. It was played out in the classrooms of William Tyndale Junior School, Islington and in the rooms of London's County Hall, home of the local authority for London, the Inner London Education Authority (ILEA).

Notes

1 Before drawing up their conclusions, members of the Plowden Committee visited 267 schools and 11 Colleges of Education, and made numerous visits to other countries.
2 Timothy Raison, for example, who was then editor of *New Society* (and was later to became a Conservative MP and Home Office Minister) had been a member of the Plowden Committee and was also deeply concerned about the Black Paper attack (Raison, 1990).

Chapter 3

William Tyndale Junior School

Another Term of Trial for the Class of '75
Allegations flew thick and fast outside the trouble-hit William Tyndale Junior school . . . of teachers smelling of drink after lunchtime pub sessions; of a child being hit on the head with a pair of scissors; of nine year olds still unable to read and write; of Left-wing subversion by the teaching staff. (Daily Express, 1975a)

William Tyndale Junior School, in Islington North London, first made dramatic national newspaper headlines in July 1975 when the school managers were 'banned' from entering the school. *The Times* led with the headline, **Teachers refuse to let managers into school for inspection**. 'The whole concept of the managerial system is under attack', complained Brian Tennant, 'chairman' of the school managers (Times, 1975a). In September 1975 when the teachers refused to cooperate with an inspection of the school by the local authority (the ILEA), the school became the topic of almost daily national coverage. 'Teachers' pawn', led the *Daily Express*, 'I'm no blackleg says boy who fled strike school' (Daily Express, 1975b). 'Parents boycott "school of shame" as teachers go back', the *Daily Telegraph* wrote. 'It's an outrage says parents' (Daily Telegraph, 1975).

During the course of the Tyndale drama, both camps in the dispute invoked different philosophical traditions, beliefs and ideologies to justify their approaches to teaching and learning. The question 'who rules our schools?' became a major issue for resolution. There was almost daily coverage of Tyndale throughout the four months in which a public investigation into events at the troubled school — the Auld Inquiry — took evidence[1]. The political and ideological battles soon made the headlines and made good newspaper copy:

Head who thought writing was obsolete (Daily Mail, 1975)

Who can mediate in the class war? (Guardian, 1975a)

A radical experiment for our schools (Financial Times, 1975)

Trotskyist Teachers' Warning to Parents (Evening News, 1975)

Children from William Tyndale School 'blacked' (Times, 1975b)

The intense media attention led to allegations that there was a 'witch-hunt' against the teachers.

Tyndale Seven complain of vicious campaign (Guardian, 1975b)

Events at Tyndale created waves — and indeed a veritable storm — which resounded not only in the world of education but on the wider national stage and which eventually reached the ears of the Prime Minister of the day, James Callaghan.

The account of events at William Tyndale presented in this chapter draws on a range of sources: the Auld Report (1976); written evidence submitted by a number of those involved in proceedings; the account of events written by a number of teachers involved (Ellis et al., 1976); a transcript of a play about events at Tyndale produced at the National Theatre (Connaughton, 1976); comprehensive press coverage from the ILEA's press cuttings service; radio coverage: and a range of contemporary articles and accounts of events. The chapter also draws on interviews with a number of those whose were involved in events, including Robin Auld who headed the Inquiry, Anne Page and Rhodes Boyson. (Appendix I contains a list of the interviewees.) As I was unable to interview any of the teachers involved, I have tried as far as possible, to allow their voice to be heard by drawing heavily on their account of events, as well as transcripts of radio interviews. I have also chosen to quote in some detail, a number of extracts from evidence provided to the Inquiry and from private papers of a number of those involved, to enable the reader to gain their own insights into events.

William Tyndale School

The William Tyndale Junior and Infants Schools were housed in premises in the St Mary's Ward of Islington, an inner city part of North London, close to the local Town Hall, and close to Fleet Street where most of the national papers were then based. The proximity of the school to Fleet Street undoubtedly contributed to the extensive press coverage. Events centred around the Junior School, although inevitably they spilled into the life of the Infant School.

The story began in the spring of 1973, with the resignation of the headteacher of the Junior School after five years of headship. According to the Inquiry, up to that time, the Junior School had a good reputation locally. The post of headteacher was advertised twice. Terry Ellis was appointed on the second round of interviews and took up his position in January 1974. However, by the time Mr Ellis had completed two terms at the school, it was in a state of crisis:

> It was in complete turmoil . . . The teaching and organization of the School was in great disorder; the content and quality of the teaching by several Staff was causing serious alarm . . . discipline throughout the school had broken down . . . ; the School's teaching Staff were divided . . . Mr Ellis and some of his Staff had lost, irretrievably, the confidence of certain of the School's Managers . . . ; many parents of children at the school had lost confidence in it and relations between Mr Ellis and some of his Staff on the one hand and many parents on the other were bad; relationships between Mr Ellis and some of his Staff . . . and Miss Hart (the headteacher of the Infants School) and the Infants School Staff . . . were very strained. (Auld, 1976, para. 838)

What had brought the school to this disastrous state of affairs within such a short space of time?

The Emerging Saga

In the Autumn term of 1973, the deputy headteacher, Irene Chowles took over as acting head in the interregnum between the retiring and newly appointed head. By all accounts it was a difficult term (not helped by the fact that 4 of the 11 staff had been newly appointed to the school in September 1973) and the school deteriorated. One of the new teachers, Brian Haddow, who had been appointed to the school to take responsibility for boys' games and school journeys, was also given the position of acting deputy headteacher to Mrs Chowles. Brian Haddow was to become be a key figure in the saga.

In January 1974, the Spring term, Terry Ellis joined the school and Mrs Chowles resumed her post as deputy head. The new headteacher (strongly supported by Brian Haddow) embarked on a series of debates about the function of schools in society and about teaching methods. According to Mrs Chowles and Dolly Walker (a part-time teacher of reading who also played a prominent part in events) Mr Haddow was committed to changing society through the children he taught: a claim which Mr Haddow himself denied. Robin Auld later concluded that:

> I am satisfied that both Mr Haddow and Mr Ellis were urging in their
> Staff discussions, the need to consider the system of teaching adopted
> by the School as a vehicle for social change. (ibid. para. 185)

Through those early days of Terry Ellis's administration, it became clear that there were deep divisions amongst the staff about the nature of schooling and about pedagogical issues. I have illustrated the conflicting philosophical and political views of some of the main protagonists by drawing on evidence given to the Inquiry and juxtaposing this with extracts from a fictional account of events at William Tyndale School, 'Sir is Winning' (Connaughton, 1977).

Views were polarized around whether the role of education was to provide working-class children with the skills needed to succeed in life, or whether it was merely a vehicle for ensuring that children conformed to societal requirements and expectations. There were fundamental disagreements amongst the staff not only about the direction in which the school should go but about how the staff, as a group, should make decisions. Mr Ellis wanted to widen democracy in the school and suggested that the position of headteacher be abolished and all decisions taken by the staff as a whole. Whilst this did not happen, a majority voting model was adopted, a form of school decision-making which Mr Ellis strongly advocated (Ellis et al., 1976, p. 17). Increasingly, those teachers who opposed the changes were marginalized. Mr Ellis made it clear to Mrs Chowles, for example, that 'he saw no significant role for her as deputy headteacher now that he had introduced what purported to be collective staff responsibility for deciding the policy and running of the school' (Auld, 1976, para. 191). Mrs Walker became ostracized as she adopted an increasingly strident attitude in her opposition to developments in the school (ibid. para. 187).

Nevertheless, changes began to take place in the organization of the school. In the second half of Mr Ellis's first term, Mr Haddow (with the agreement of Mr Ellis) introduced a 'twenty activity options' scheme for his class. Children could choose from a range of activities from English work and Mathematics, to football, modelling and tie-dying which extended beyond his classroom to a number of other areas in the school (ibid. paras. 195–98). The scheme was designed to promote freedom of choice and individualized learning, and both Terry Ellis and Brian Haddow believed that through the scheme children would become self-motivated and therefore successful and active learners. But the options scheme, as many of the other changes at Tyndale, was poorly planned and badly executed. Neither parents, nor other teachers in the school had been informed, or involved in the reorganization (despite

'Sir is Winning' (A fictional account of events at Tyndale Connaughton, 1997)

Scene 7: the staff room . . .

Dolly Walker: Schools are for schooling. What else?

Terry Ellis: Depends what you mean by schooling.

Brian Haddow: And after 'schooling' is over, what then?

Dolly: University, getting a good . . .

Teacher: That's rubbish. The amount of working class kids going to University is proportionately just as low today as ever before. And the amount of kids leaving schools unable to find work is at an all time high.

Brian: So what are we educating them for? For the dole queue? Are we to send them out unaware how the system works?

Dolly: I knew we'd get round to politics.

Brian: Well we must ask fundamental questions. Our kids here at this school come from backgrounds — fathers (out of work . . .)

Dolly: Not all the children in this school are from depressed backgrounds, Brian. We have middle class children too you know.

Brian: Yes, kids of trendy middle class parents who want them to get as much out of the system as possible.

Dolly: What's wrong with that?

Brian: Nothing.

Teacher: As long as it's not at the expense of the deprived kid.

Brian: Right.

Terry: A choice has to be made. And I think we ought always to come down on the side of the deprived.

Scene 23: the school corridor . . .

Manager (1): We've heard you're having problems. Some children appear to be having difficulty with your option scheme. In fact, I heard some parents were considering withdrawing their children.

Terry Ellis: Who told you that?

Manager (2): Doesn't matter who.

Manager (1): I think perhaps we should have a meeting about it all, with the parents.

Manager (2): And with us the managers.

Terry: We've already had a parents' meeting; where we explained all about the options schemes. All it needs now is time for it to work.

Manager (2): We as managers have a right to know what's going on here.

Terry: Sure, but in the meantime let us, the teachers, get on with the job, Eh?

Evidence from the Auld Inquiry
(Auld, 1976, paras. 181, 183, 184 and 186)

Mr Ellis

Mr Ellis claimed in evidence at the Inquiry that he was firmly of the view that the educational aims and teaching methods of a school should be determined by the teaching staff as a whole, and that, if possible, there should be full agreement by the teaching staff as a whole about such matters.

From the start he introduced regular staff meetings at which the teachers were encouraged to, and did, discuss the educational direction that the School should take . . .

This new approach was welcomed by all of the Staff at the outset . . .

However, . . . they generated into heated philosophical debates . . .

The main protagonists on each side were Mr Haddow and Mrs Walker . . .

Mr Haddow

Mr Haddow was for a radical change to a less formal teaching system where the children had a much greater say in their learning and in the way in which the School itself was organized.

Mrs Walker

Mrs Walker was, and is convinced that the function of a junior school education is to equip children with the basic skills which they can then go on to use in their secondary education and in their adult life as tools for making their way in society and forming their own judgements about it.

Her view is that without the ability to use such skills a child is deprived of the main stimulus to learn and to develop 'his' own interests and abilities. Such basic skills, in her view, cannot be taught to children without a well-defined and disciplined method of teaching in which the children are firmly directed by the teacher.

the commitment to democracy). The Inquiry, concluded that Mr Haddow had approached the changes in a 'sanguine and rather casual manner' and as a consequence of the haste, within a short time, a number of the parents had noticed a deterioration in the attitude and behaviour of their children and began to voice their concerns (ibid. para. 200).

By the end of Mr Ellis's first term, the school managers were beginning to have some worries about the changes which were taking place in the school, and about the reactions of parents. Elizabeth Hoodless, a school manager recalled her first meeting of the governing body of Tyndale.

> Arising from the minutes Robin Mabey (one of the school managers prominent in the Tyndale affair) asked how the problem of juniors dropping milk bottles onto the nursery had been dealt with. The headmaster assured the managers that all was well. So he was pressed for how this solution had been achieved, and it had been achieved by asking the dairy to deliver packets instead of bottles. This did not seem to me to be the way to run a school. (BBC, 1989)

Despite these concerns, the school nevertheless had achieved some successes. A school steel band had been set up which won an ILEA prize for excellence. The steel band did much to raise the confidence and self-esteem of its members and, as a consequence, the reading levels of a number of the children involved in the band improved substantially.

During the summer term of 1974, Mr Ellis's second term at the school, the staff room debates became even more heated. Discussions focused around the role of the headteacher and pupil/teacher relationships. Several members of staff wanted to extend democracy further in the school and to remove what they saw as some of the barriers between staff and pupils. One practical way of doing this was to open the staff room to children. Despite bitter opposition from some of the staff this change was introduced. As the term progressed, views became even more polarized between those staff who saw themselves as promoting freedom of choice and free expression (Mr Haddow and Mr Ellis and a nucleus of staff) and those who saw themselves as promoting basic skills and discipline (largely Mrs Walker). There was a third group of staff, which included Mrs Chowles, who retreated from the increasingly virulent debate to the relative sanctuary of their own classrooms (ibid. paras. 237–8).

The personalities, conflicting aspirations and actions of particular individuals undoubtedly contributed to the growing difficulties at Tyndale.

Peter Newsam (who was to become the administrative leader of the ILEA in the wake of Tyndale) had no doubt when I interviewed him of the commitment and concern of the staff at Tyndale. Their refusal, towards the end of the saga, to allow the school to be inspected ultimately placed them in a totally unacceptable position. In his view also, Terry Ellis's attempt to reconstruct the role of the headteacher as school 'convener' rather than 'head', was not out of line with that of many London primary headteachers at the time. Where Terry Ellis differed was in the scope of his ambitions and how he went about achieving them. He was not an effective leader.

> He was a good and thoughtful teacher but he was not a good headteacher. He had a lot on his hands and instead of moving carefully, he moved too fast.

Mr Ellis failed to achieve any unity, or a common sense of purpose amongst his staff.

Brian Haddow was a significant 'player' and the Inquiry concluded that 'of all the teaching Staff referred to in this Report, he had the most profound influence upon the organization and teaching methods and attitudes that were adopted at the Junior School in 1974 and 1975' (ibid. para. 131). Views about Brian Haddow and his role in events at Tyndale were mixed. One interviewee described him as a 'hard person, a trouble-maker and an ideologue'. However, in the view of school manager Elizabeth Hoodless, Brian Haddow was a gifted teacher.

> He was an extremely talented teacher who had developed very innovative methods in the classrooms and then tried to persuade other teachers to follow him. His methods were very fruitful because of his high levels of talent but for the average teachers it was too difficult to cope with and they did not. (BBC, 1989)

Another key player was Mrs Walker, a vociferous critic of Brian Haddow and Terry Ellis who subjected her colleagues at Tyndale to intense personal attack[2].

Despite all their differences, the staff were united in the need to introduce a new reading group scheme in which all members of staff would take responsibility for a group of children with similar abilities. The new scheme began just before the end of the summer term but did not survive long. It was introduced without proper planning and appeared to be beyond the skills and experience of a number of the staff involved, some of whom did not follow through on the scheme. Disenchantment amongst staff was such that one member of staff wrote on her black-board, 'I hate reading groups'. The Inquiry concluded that the failure of the reading scheme disturbed many children and contributed to a general climate of malaise and boredom in the school (ibid. paras. 248–50).

Criticisms began to erupt from a range of sources during that summer term. Critics included Miss Hart (headteacher of the infant school) who was concerned about the breakdown of behaviour of children in the junior school. Mr Ellis rejected Miss Hart's criticisms on the grounds that 'she had sold out to the middle classes' (ibid. para. 114). Both parents and school managers also expressed their concerns to the headteacher but according to the Inquiry, their views were dismissed as inappropriate and challenging to the legitimate professional interests of teachers (ibid. paras. 251–60). The district inspector received further complaints about the school and discussed these with Mr Ellis but the situation continued to deteriorate (ibid. para. 306).

The Debate

At the beginning of May 1974, Mrs Walker decided to make public her views about the school. She proposed to call a parents' meeting to discuss matters and produced a written paper for staff entitled, 'Commentary on William Tyndale School' in which she described the school in the following trenchant terms:

> Chaos and anarchy are in possession. Discipline is frowned on as 'old-fashioned'. Children are being seduced to behave in ways which are detrimental to them, both in their progress in learning anything and in producing anti-social behaviour . . . The fault for this state of affairs is constantly placed on the home background — whereas it is almost entirely due to the School atmosphere. (Too true — Abandon hope all ye who enter here!) Terry Ellis is the biggest buck-passer I have ever met . . . Brain Haddow talks of Children's Rights. What about the Right to a decent Education? . . . I feel these children and their parents are being poorly served by this school . . . (ibid. para. 260)

Mrs Walker also voiced her concerns to the district inspector and to the chair of governors. She had already met with Rhodes Boyson, at that time a newly appointed Member of Parliament and a leading voice in the Conservative critique of state education. Mrs Walker's relationship with Rhodes Boyson, and her apparent involvement in the 'Black Paper' cause, became a further source of bitterness between her and other members of staff at the school. Rhodes Boyson later described to me how Mrs Walker had first come to him when he was a headteacher at Highbury Grove School. 'She was concerned that no real teaching was taking place and that there was no discipline in the school.' He saw the dispute at Tyndale as having grown out of the political convictions and activities of a left-wing group within the National Union of Teachers 'rank and file'.

> By and large they were head bangers concerned with ending the system . . . The teachers at Tyndale did what others did. They weren't a communist cell and in some ways they were the least dangerous of the lot.

At about this time, Mrs Walker produced another paper entitled, 'A criticism of the "Free Choice" method of education based on total children's rights as at William Tyndale Junior School' which later became known as, 'Mrs Walker's Black Paper'.

A criticism of the 'Free Choice' method of education based on total children's rights as at William Tyndale Junior School, 1974

Mrs Walker's 'Black Paper'

Whatever the supposed merits of a total free choice environment for children in school may be, it is evident that it also has some very serious drawbacks in that:

1. It is divisive in effect . . . It divides children from parents and from parental control and home discipline . . . It divides parents from teachers because there is no agreement about how the children are handled . . . It is particularly divisive for the child who is backward in his learning . . .

2. It fails to provide an environment for steady learning and the development of good learning habits. 'Free choice' inevitably results in a more or less disorganised, haphazard state of affairs in the classroom . . . It particularly increases the level of disturbance and distraction . . . It provides no incentive to learn . . . No goals are set and there is no stimulation to achievement . . . the child with a bent for academic learning does not have this satisfaction . . . The less intelligent child, or the less able child who has emotional problems, or the sensitive child who cannot work in an atmosphere of noise, or the backward child who needs special help — all these are at an even greater disadvantage compared to their tougher integrated or able schoolmates . . . This system benefits the teachers who are no longer obliged to prepare lessons, mark books, teach subjects, or even supervise the children to some degree . . .

---

3. It is based on a number of fallacies . . . that children dislike learning under the guidance of a teacher . . . that children don't like discipline . . . that freedom is something one can have and exercise without responsibility . . . that there is great educational value in setting up a situation in which children can learn to choose and thereby choose to learn . . . that all children are . . . happier under a total free choice . . . system . . . that a do-as-you-please policy in school is somehow not the same as spoiling the child at home.

. . . The road to progress for our children is through education . . . that is why . . . the 'trend' in education towards withdrawing the teacher's help and leaving the children to motivate themselves . . . is particularly harmful and unsuitable in a so-called 'deprived' area like Islington. (Walker, 1974)

Mrs Walker's link with Rhodes Boyson heightened tensions in the school and later led some staff to perceive events at Tyndale as a conspiracy of the political Right. Mrs Walker was seen by her colleagues as a strong advocate of the Black Paper movement, supported in this by Rhodes Boyson.

Although the staff labelled her document in July 1974 the 'Black Paper', (Mrs Walker) claimed in the Inquiry that she knew little of the theories of Black Paper writers and their sympathisers. Yet she was in constant cordial contact with a leading Black Paper figure, Boyson, from the time she made her first attack on her colleagues' philosophy until the beginning of the Inquiry. The document she produced at the inquiry totalling 8,000 words, are an accurate summary of many aspects of Black Paper theory. (Ellis et al., 1976, p. 40)

If Mrs Walker's views could be described as out of the Black Paper mould, how then could the views of Mr Ellis and his colleagues be categorized? Mr Haddow saw education as a means to tackling social disadvantage (a view Margaret Thatcher shared to some degree during her period as Secretary of State for Education — see Chapter 2).

Mr Haddow saw the new system as being of particular benefit to the socially deprived and emotionally disturbed children in that, according to him, they were able to develop far greater self-sufficiency in this free atmosphere than under the more conventional classroom system . . . As to the brighter and more academic children, Mr Haddow's evidence was that they continued to work in much the same way as before . . . He did recognize, however, that there was a 'middle group' . . . who did not benefit from the new scheme and . . . tended to drift. (Auld, para. 199)

The Inquiry concluded that Mr Haddow and Mr Ellis encouraged staff to adopt a progressive teaching approach which put the interests of the child at the centre:

> It has the elements of cooperative or team teaching; it is 'child-centred'. It also involves . . . a 'non-confrontational' approach, by which I understand that the teacher does not try to force a child to learn when the child is unwilling to do so, but indirectly over a period of time arouses the child's interest so that he or she gradually develops an interest and a willingness to learn. (ibid. para. 240)

Rhodes Boyson was later to define progressive education in somewhat more caustic terms:

> Often you can define something most clearly by defining the opposite. The opposite of progressive education is structured education where the teacher is a teacher and he comes into the classroom and he says 'sit down' and (the pupils) all sit down facing the right way, and he says, 'we are doing this and we are going to learn something'. You see school as moving from one part of instruction to another which is examined and which they are going to keep for the rest of their lives.
>
> The opposite is the idea like a bud of a flower, almost 'Rousseauesque' that all you need to do is free people and they will then become the learners themselves. The child is desperate for knowledge and development, and thus you do not have a structure for learning. Each child does what it wants to do, possibly playing table tennis with another in the corridor to disrupt everyone else in the school, but that is the *crie de cœur* of the child that should be encouraged. There is no set pattern, it is just a question of the teacher following whatever the child can do, even to the child's destruction. (BBC, 1989)

In the summer of 1976, Terry Ellis, Brian Haddow and two other teachers from Tyndale (Jackie McWhirter and Dorothy McColgan) were to put their account of events into writing in a book on Tyndale (Ellis et al., 1976). They did not see the conflict as being in terms of progressive versus traditional education but argued instead that 'liberal' education, as promoted at the time by the ILEA, was simply not working. The liberal philosophy espoused by Plowden was laced with contradictions and competing expectations of teachers. On the one hand, they were still expected to exert control over children, at the same time, however, children were to be empowered to take control of their own learning. Terry Ellis and his colleagues attempted to deconstruct the notion of progressive education articulated in Plowden to create an alternative perspective.

The Tyndale Philosophy

To represent the Tyndale conflict as, in part, a battle between progress-ive and traditional education is an over-simplification. If Walker's view was radical, in its original sense of wishing to make root changes, so were those of her many opponents on the staff. She was not just traditional, they were not just progressive. Both sides found much to criticise in the liberal education view adopted by the ILEA image-makers and the Tyndale managers. The staff were attacked by those who thought themselves pro-gressive and the managers accused them of bringing progressive education into disrepute.

What was the philosophy that provoked such wrath?

Much might appear to be embraced by the term progressive, if that word itself had not become virtually meaningless . . . The Tyndale staff were aware of the contradictions in much so-called progressive educa-tion, how it is often simply traditional education in disguise, the means more indirect, the manner more showy, the ends exactly the same. They knew that many forward looking ideas thrown out in the balmy air of the 1960s were in the process of freezing to death in the cold, uncomforting climate of today, that many teachers who had spoken so resoundingly then of fluidity in the curriculum and responding to kids were now re-treating into cautious mutterings about structure and maintaining standards. In many ways, the staff were seeking to carry through to logical conclu-sion many ideas that had seemed exciting in the post-Plowden era, while breaking through the progressive contradictions, by reaching out to more radical perspectives and methods . . .

Schools have always been concerned with social control. In many it is an amalgam of obsessions — with uniforms, length of hair, bad language, religious sanctions and petty secular rules. Schooling is a mat-ter of conditioning those schooled into the acceptance of such modes of thinking and acting as society deems proper. The teacher, as part of the apparatus of control, has assumed the roles of law-giver, moraliser, indoctrinator, communicator of the acceptable views and taboos of the tribe — a strict father or mother backed up by the system as long as those in control think the job is being done effectively.

The ferment of ideas in the 1960s threatened to crack this mould. Active rather than passive learning became the accepted theory, subject divisions were blurred: greater emphasis was placed on human relation-ships and social development; classrooms were arranged as informal work-shops, no longer as schooling boxes dominated by a centrally important teacher. The means and much of the content of schooling was changed — though not overnight, not in many schools.

Content and method have a great influence on the role of the teacher. It is more difficult to adopt a dominating stance in an informal classroom, or to assume an obvious controlling and conditioning position where pupils' views are thought to be important. Had teachers taken the new methods to their logical conclusion and questioned the ends to which they were educating as they were now questioning the means, a change in the teachers' role might have taken place . . .

The teacher, who had been a strict parent, now becomes the occasionally severe aunt or uncle. Many have remarked on how much more strenuous such teaching is. This is quite understandable, being crafty all day is a tiring business. The real motives of schooling and the controlling role of the teacher have been gently evaded. The contradictions have been papered over with triple mounted pictures and production line creative writing. This moribund prettiness devoid of all motive except the transference of middle class values to working class children, has been embraced by many schools, especially those with a strong middle class parental element.

The Tyndale staff were trying to break through these contradictions when their efforts were smothered . . . Their philosophy was democratic, egalitarian and anti-sexist, it was concerned with children's social development, with their individual needs and achievements; it was geared to activity not passivity made no false distinction between work and play; rejected arbitrary standards of attainment and behaviour; asserted the necessity for a wide range of choices the involvement of children in their own community, and exercise of positive discrimination towards the disadvantaged and encouraged children to think for themselves and gain the confidence to dominate material presented to them. Children were encouraged to ask questions, not conditioned to obey orders, as Ellis emphasised at the inquiry. Maybe this was why sir had such a hard time winning when the inspectors took over the school in September 1975? (Ellis et al., 1976, pp. 42–5)

The analysis presented by staff at Tyndale of progressive education corresponds with the critique of Sharp and Green (described in Chapter 2). Both highlight tensions and inconsistencies in progressive education, its voluntaristic and individualistic nature, and both share a view that it had become a new form of social control. But in trying to play out what they saw as the logical extension of the progressive tradition, the Tyndale staff failed to reconcile their aspirations with the practical realities of planning, progression and challenge and to accept that boundaries needed to be set, about behaviour for example, an issue which is discussed more fully later in the chapter.

As the ideological conflict was played out at Tyndale, the acrimony amongst staff reached new heights and the disruptions within the school escalated. Relationships between staff and school managers became even more strained when a number of the managers visited the school to look in some detail at what was happening. Attitudes became polarized following an informal meeting between three of the managers, Terry Ellis and Brian Haddow, in which the managers argued that the staff needed to hold a meeting with parents to discuss changes in the school and parental concerns. In response Mr Ellis and Mr Haddow (the staff representative on the school managers' board) challenged the right of the managers to question the educational policies of the staff (ibid. para. 294). The growing dispute between the managers and the teachers now became a central element in the conflict.

The 'Grey' Area of School Governance

In the mid 1970s, school managers had been given 'oversight' of the school. What this meant in practice became a central element in the conflict at Tyndale. For the two decades following the 1944 Education Act, the role of school managers had been somewhat ill-defined. With the post-war establishment of secondary education, local education authorities were obliged under the terms of the Act to appoint school managers, but there was no requirement to appoint managers for individual schools. By the mid-sixties, only 21 out of the 78 county boroughs which had responsibility for local education had set up governing bodies for each school (Tomlinson, 1993). The Inner London Education Authority was one of those.

In exercising their oversight, school managers were expected to be generally supportive of what was happening in schools and particularly supportive of the headteacher. During this period, according to Gerald Grace (1995), English schools acquired a relatively large degree of pedagogical and cultural autonomy from which headteachers, rather than school managers, benefited. The content of the curriculum, modes of assessment, teaching and learning became *de facto* the responsibility of teachers and, in particular, that of headteachers. Although some formal power was vested with the school managers, it was only in extreme circumstances — such as Tyndale — that this was put to the test and questions about the autonomy of heads, or the authority of governors, raised.

At a meeting for school managers organized by the ILEA in July 1974, two of the managers including the then chair (Mrs Burnett) tried unsuccessfully to clarify these governance issues and to bring their growing concerns about the school to the attention of the ILEA. Mrs Burnett asked how managers should exercise their duty of overseeing the conduct and curriculum of the school and in what detail. She was answered in the following terms by Mrs Chaplin, an ILEA politician who was chair of one of the main committees of the Authority:

> Managers shall, in consultation with the headteacher control the conduct and curriculum, the internal organisation, management and discipline of the school . . . **It is, therefore, quite proper for the managers to ask the head for information** about (for example) the curriculum and ask how the school is run . . . they can express a view . . . (but) they cannot order the head to do any of those things . . .
>
> I hope that all managers will make it their business really to find out the sorts of things that are happening in their schools . . . **But I want to stress that the managers and governors must not tell the head what to do.** . . . It is the duty of the managers to know exactly what is going on in a school. (Auld, para. 348)

Mrs Burnett also put the following question:

> If it should occur that there is a serious division of opinion on certain aspects of a school between the governing or managing board and the head, and it looks as though they are not going to resolve this difficulty, could you give me some guidance as to what happens next?

Mrs Chaplin replied:

> I think the answer is no. . . . (ibid. para. 349)

This exchange illustrates the 'grey areas' of school governance and the lack of clarity about the role of school managers which added further complexities to the Tyndale saga. The ILEA did not provide sufficient guidance to the school managers about their role. Mrs Burnett had asked for guidance in the event of a dispute between governors and a headteacher. She had been given none[3].

Relationships with Parents

As the difficulties increased between the teachers and the school managers, so relationships between teachers and parents became even more strained. Parents began to question the behaviour of teachers and to challenge some of the practices within the school. On 13 June, a parents–teacher meeting was held to discuss the teachers' London-wide pay claim. Staff explained to parents why they had taken unofficial industrial action but parents were critical of this and of the failure to give parents sufficient warning of their actions. Parents also raised their concerns about the quality of education being offered by the school and called for an urgent meeting on this matter. That meeting took place on 9 July.

With the agreement of the chair of the school managers the teachers had produced a brief paper on the aims of education at Tyndale which was intended for discussion at that 9 July meeting. These points were as follows:

Aims of William Tyndale School: 5 points

1 To encourage all children to live together in school harmony.
2 To encourage all children to think for themselves and make their own decisions about their learning and their lives.
3 To ensure that each child can read, express himself/herself clearly and thoughtfully in language.
4 To ensure that each child is well grounded in basic mathematics.
5 To provide a wide choice of activities and interests for a child to experience and enjoy in a stable environment.

It is difficult to disagree with the declared aims of William Tyndale School as expressed in the teachers' note presented to that meeting. The problems and difficulties lay in how those ideas had been translated into practice, and the lack of consensus about those plans with all those involved. However, because of events at the meeting, the ideas were never discussed with parents. Prior to the 9 July meeting, Mrs Walker had circulated her 'Black Paper' to a number of parents and just before the meeting commenced, she also placed copies of the paper on all the seats. Both actions were taken without the knowledge of the other staff, or the chair of governors, and served to raise the temperature of the meeting at an early stage.

The meeting was acrimonious. Criticisms about the so-called 'free choice' system at Tyndale were expressed by a number of parents, as well as by Mrs Walker herself. During the course of the meeting, Mr Haddow and four of the teachers walked out which 'produced complete uproar for a time' (ibid. para. 387). Mrs Walker's behaviour at the meeting served to create even greater bitterness between her and colleagues. They were equally bitter at the failure of the ILEA to discipline her on this and other matters, and the ILEA was later censured by the Inquiry for failing to tackle Mrs Walker's behaviour.

> . . . The Authority's administrative machinery failed to deal properly with the problems of Mrs Walker . . . (It) presented the problem . . . as being essentially an issue between Mr Ellis and the majority of his Staff on the one hand, and Mrs Walker on the other. (ibid. para. 409)

On 11 July, two days after the meeting, the Divisional Inspector, Mr Rice; sent a report to County Hall about Tyndale in which he gave no information about the parent/teachers' meeting. The Auld Inquiry concluded that this failure to pass on the information was one of the many serious errors in the conduct of the whole affair.

By the end of the summer term (Mr Ellis's second in the school), discipline had began to be a major problem in the school. At the Inquiry it was suggested that a general slackness of attitude had developed which included staff arriving late. This coupled with the introduction of Mr Haddow's class options schemes and the failure of the reading group scheme had contributed to this state of affairs. School managers met with the Divisional Inspector to express their growing concerns about developments within the school.

The falling school roll in the junior school (at a time when numbers were expanding in the infant school) gives some indication of the impact of events on the attitudes of parents in the local community. Parents who felt that they could not influence what was happening at Tyndale used the only veto that they had and voted with their feet. Many transferred their children to other junior schools, or transferred from the infants school to neighbouring junior schools. The dramatic drop in the school roll is shown as follows:

September 1973 — 230 pupils
January 1974 — 220 pupils
September 1974 — 155 pupils
Easter 1975 — 144 pupils
September 1975 — 114 pupils

The academic year 1974–75 commenced and the teachers decided to introduce a 'co-operative teaching scheme' for second and third year children. Once again, the scheme lacked adequate planning and was further weakened by poor preparation and record keeping (ibid. paras. 462–74). There was disruption and time-wasting as children moved around the school from one activity to another and, although the scheme had been designated a co-operative teaching system, teachers adopted their own styles and approaches which caused confusion for some of the children. The Inquiry concluded that although some children, particularly those who were most disturbed, had benefited from it, 'the scheme was ill-conceived and badly run' by Mr Haddow and his team of teachers (ibid. para. 587). Had it been properly planned, however, it could have succeeded (ibid. para. 475).

Throughout the Autumn term of 1974, relationships between the teachers and the school managers continued to deteriorate and a number of managers visited — or attempted to visit — the school on official business. The legitimacy of the managers to make these visits — and the manner in which they were made — became a further source of contention. The teachers claimed that the visits of the school managers were peremptory and that there was an organized political campaign against the school (ibid. para. 547). The managers grew increasingly more anxious about the condition of the school (ibid. para. 588).

Views from the Sidelines

In the Spring term of 1975, Anne Page, Islington Council's representative on the ILEA (she had replaced Jack Straw, who later became an MP and Home Secretary) began to be concerned about developments at Tyndale. Anne Page had came to the UK from South Africa where she had become politicized as a student in Cape Town. She had become a local councillor and Islington representative on the ILEA because of her experience as a parent. 'I was concerned with the quality of what was being offered, it never occurred to me not to use the local schools, I just wanted them to be better' she told me. Anne Page saw the Tyndale dispute as being about ideology and about practice. Teachers at Tyndale had become more interested in ideology than teaching. Non-hierarchical management had became much more important than the needs of children. But what really mattered was the practice and the attitude of the teachers. In her view, both had been found wanting at Tyndale[4].

Anne Page recalled examples of the poor behaviour of junior school children: dropping milk bottles out of the first floor windows onto the playground of the infant's school below, swearing at teachers. On one occasion, children had been taken to nearby Highbury Fields on a school outing but several had been left behind and had had to find their own way back to the school. (I always remember the 'words of wisdom' from the headteacher in the first school in which I worked when I was about to embark on my first school trip, 'Whatever you do, come back with the same number you left with.') In Anne Page's view, the pursuit of free expression had taken over at William Tyndale. She contrasted Tyndale with the White Lion Free School which operated successfully nearby at the time, with an apparently similar philosophy.

> The White Lion Free School by contrast was very concerned with both rights and responsibilities. Bad behaviour was simply not allowed to go unchallenged . . . The White Lion Free School was careful but Tyndale was careless.

As her concerns about the school grew, Anne Page tried unsuccessfully to get the ILEA to take action. She twice suggested that the school be inspected in order to analyse the problems and identify an appropriate course of action. The Inquiry later concluded that the William Tyndale Junior School would have benefited from an early inspection.

The Battle Escalates

In early 1975, the school managers stepped up their campaign to persuade the ILEA to intervene in the school. Having (in their view) been ignored by official channels, they used Labour Party informal networks to bring their concerns to the attention of County Hall politicians, particularly the Reverend Harvey Hinds, Chair of the School Committee. Despite these attempts to galvanize the ILEA into action, the Authority still failed to act and some of the managers set about organizing a 'secret' petition about the school. This petition and the manner in which it was collected undoubtedly served to bring about the final estrangement between the managers and the teachers (ibid. paras. 676–81) and in May 1975, the managers passed the following motion:

> We the Managers of William Tyndale Schools note with concern:
> (i)   the petition circulating in the neighbourhood about the school;
> (ii)   the rapidly declining rolls;
> and call upon the ILEA to take urgent steps to restore public confidence in the schools including consideration of reorganisation as a JM and I school. (ibid. para. 685)

Staff responded to this motion by taking measures to oppose the transfer of children from William Tyndale to other junior schools in the area (ibid. paras. 704–7). They also appealed to the ILEA for help against the managers (ibid. para. 689). In June and July various attempts were made by the Authority to mediate, but matters continued to escalate. The teachers refused to allow managers to visit the school during school hours (ibid. paras. 716–28) on the grounds that:

> The resolution of 19 May was tantamount to a vote of no confidence in the work of the school. We therefore feel that any ensuing visit can only be in the nature of an inspection in order to justify this belief by attempting to gather information against us. (ibid. para. 272)

Some of the managers responded by testing out their right to visit the school and when they were barred from the school, they involved the national press (ibid. paras. 740–744). It was the banning of the school managers from the school which hit the headlines, creating inevitable difficulties for the reconciliation meeting which the ILEA had planned. The 'chairman' of the school's managers, Brian Tennant, described the teachers' ban in the following terms:

> The whole concept of the managerial system is under attack. The authority (the ILEA) must decide the relationship of managers vis-a-vis the school. It is extremely short-sighted of teachers not to allow managers in on the education of the children. You cannot sweep things under the carpet. (Times, 1975a)

Staff justified the ban on the basis that the managers had already passed a motion (which was virtually a vote of 'no confidence' in the staff) and that: 'Any managerial visit could only involve a search for evidence to reinforce and give credence to that resolution' (Ellis et al., 1976, p. 99)

At this stage, the ILEA suggested an inspection of the infant and junior schools. The junior school teachers rejected this proposal on the grounds that they wanted an inquiry by the Secretary of State into the conduct of the managers. The Authority ordered an inspection. The teachers went on strike and opened an alternative school in a neighbouring building, where they continued for some two weeks with 24 pupils. Meanwhile an 'inspection' of sorts (not a full inspection in the absence of the teachers and a number of the pupils) was carried out. Terry Ellis and his colleagues later described the inspection in the following terms:

> Among the documents relating to the first inspection report on Tyndale in September 1975 is a memorandum by Inspector Norman Geddes. It is not a report, but a description of his experiences with the class he had to teach when the teachers were on strike. He performs the unique act of inspecting his own teaching and finding it good. He battles against his rebellious pupils, and gains control. The most striking phrase he uses is, by the second afternoon there was a definite impression that Sir was winning. This unmasks a set of assumptions about the teacher's role. How does Sir see himself? And if sir is winning, whom is he fighting, and above all who is losing? (Ellis et al., 1976, p. 44)

The teachers' opposition to the inspection and their strike action incensed the managers who were determined to find ways of keeping the teachers from returning to the school. They passed the following motion:

Resolved the Managers seek assurance from the ILEA that the teachers at present at William Tyndale Junior School (i.e. the temporary teachers brought in to teach when the core staff went on strike) should continue until the Inquiry had reported, and the Authority be asked not to accept any return to work to William Tyndale Junior School by the striking teachers until that time. (Auld, para. 811)

An interim report on the school was produced by the Inspectorate. The chair of the school managers passed this report to the press. A meeting between the Leader of the ILEA, Sir Ashley Bramall took place on the day that newspapers carried the dramatic headlines **Rebel School is Slammed, School of Shame**. The following week the teachers returned to the school, cooperated in the inspection and agreed to give evidence at the Public Inquiry which was to be set up and was due to begin at the end of October.

Notes

1 The composition and brief of the Inquiry are discussed in Chapter 4.
2 According to an interviewee, another influential teacher at Tyndale was Mrs McColgan. 'She was an excellent teacher but as a committed member of the SWP (Social Workers Party) and an experienced organizer, she had a strong political influence on events at the school.'
3 Mrs Burnett continued to seek some resolution of the problems of Tyndale over many months. Giving evidence to the Inquiry, she claimed that anger that the Tyndale teachers had called upon other schools to refuse to accept children from Tyndale had finally driven her, in the summer of 1975, to organize a petition about the school and to speak to the education correspondent of *The Times*. 'Somebody had to do something about the children . . . I had contacted the divisional office until I was blue in the face'. *The Times* story appeared on the day of a crucial meeting about the school which was an unfortunate coincidence and Mrs Burnett apologized to the Inquiry for the intemperate way in which she had described events at Tyndale (Times, 1975).
4 In one of the many pieces written at the time about Tyndale, Peter Wilby argued that the secret of success in good progressive schools was more not less structure — an issue discussed in Chapter 2. Schools such as Prior Weston Primary School, London (with headteacher Henry Pluckrose at the helm) were beacons of progressive teaching at the time because they recognized that 'informal teaching requires hard work, careful preparation, skill, patience and good record-keeping' (Wilby, 1975).

Chapter 4

The Fallout from Tyndale

The summer following the (Auld) Inquiry, we were on holiday on the Isle of Wight. I had arranged to meet Margaret Jay (daughter of Jim Callaghan) at a nearby beach. We sailed there in our dinghy and as we rounded the headland, we saw a huge group of people — lots of the family. As we landed, I was hailed by Virginia Bottomley (Margaret Jay's cousin who became a Conservative Minister) who had a book on her lap. 'I'm delighted to see you' she said, 'I'm just reading the Auld Report, it's a gripping tale'. (Anne Page, Islington Councillor and Member of the Inner London Education Authority who featured in the Auld Report (the Public Inquiry into the William Tyndale Junior School))

My reading of the Auld Report took place some twenty years later in the summer of 1996. The report was the product of an extended Public Inquiry which highlighted the dilemmas and power struggles of those that had been drawn into the conflict at William Tyndale School. It is still — as Virginia Bottomley said so many years ago — a gripping tale: an account of a complex and painful story which unfolded over a period of eighteen months or so, and touched the lives of many people. As with any good detective novel, or Shakespearean tragedy, the intensity of the drama causes the reader to ask the 'if only' questions. 'If only' we ask, as we read 'Romeo and Juliet', the Italian postal system had been efficient. 'If only' Friar Lawrence had been more decisive. 'If only' Juliet had woken up a little sooner.

In looking at the real life drama of Tyndale, the 'if only' list is endless. 'If only' Terry Ellis (the headteacher) had planned the changes in the school more carefully and had been less dogmatic. 'If only' Dolly Walker (the Tyndale teacher most opposed to the changes) had been less intransigent and had not been so keen to find common cause with the 'Black Paperites' of the day. 'If only' the school managers had held back a little longer from talking to the media. 'If only' the Divisional Inspector had ensured that the Inner London Education Authority, which was responsible for William Tyndale, had intervened at an earlier stage.

The Auld Inquiry

In October 1975, Robin Auld QC was appointed by the Reverend Harvey Hinds, Chair of the Schools Sub-Committee of the ILEA, to conduct a Public Inquiry into the teaching, organization and management of William Tyndale Junior and Infants School, Islington. Sir Ashley Bramall, political Leader of the ILEA, had thought that the complex set of problems raised by Tyndale could be best resolved by a legal approach. No one involved in Tyndale, from the politicians to the legal representatives themselves, envisaged that the Inquiry would escalate as it did. Four ILEA members had initially been appointed to serve as members of that Inquiry but as the complexity of the issues, and the projected length of the Inquiry grew, Robin Auld QC was asked to conduct proceedings on his own. Two non-elected members of the ILEA, Dora Loftus (a Labour Party organizer) and George Carter (a headteacher), were appointed to act as advisors.

The Inquiry opened on 27 October 1975 and continued until 10 February 1976, with almost daily press coverage. The findings were published in July 1976. During the course of the Inquiry, evidence was heard from 107 witnesses during 62 days and 9 evenings. Six hundred documents were also submitted in written evidence. The total cost of the Inquiry was £55,000 of which some £50,000 was paid in legal fees. Most of these costs were later recouped from sales of the Inquiry report. The Inner London Education Authority met the cost of representation of the bulk of the witnesses (staff from the school and the governors) and also covered the replacement staffing costs for all the junior school staff during the hearing and up to the publication of the report. The various parties at the Inquiry were represented by a total of eleven barristers. The conduct of the Inquiry was exemplary but there are issues to be asked about whether a judicial hearing which replicates a courtroom is the best way of resolving such issues. To some closely involved in the Inquiry, it was the only way through the morass. As one interviewee put it to me, 'So many careers were at stake'. To others, the Inquiry was a rather large hammer to crack the small nut of a school[1].

Of the many involved in Tyndale, few escaped final censure.

The Classroom Despots
Have teachers as a group become so powerful that no one wants to argue with them? (Evening Standard, 1976)

Managers, ILEA and staff all blamed for Tyndale 'Chaos'
Teachers at the William Tyndale Junior school, Islington where scores of parents withdrew their children last year . . . paid such attention to

their own professional status and ideologies that they almost ignored the needs of children. (Daily Telegraph, 1976)

The Tragedy of William Tyndale (Observer, 18 July 1976)

Tyndale School Bosses Resign
The managers of the William Tyndale junior school in Islington who were criticised in the recently published Auld report . . . resigned last night, and parents threatened to sabotage the future of the school. (Guardian, 21 July 1976)

Anne Page was one of the exceptions. 'I am satisfied', said Robin Auld 'that Mrs Anne Page . . . has acted throughout in a responsible way in relation to the problems of William Tyndale School' (Auld, 1976, para. 305). The teachers were criticized for their intransigence, lack of planning and lack of responsiveness to parents. The local authority was criticized for having no policies on the standards of attainment which primary schools should aim for; for failing to discipline Mrs Walker; and for failing to intervene at an earlier stage.

The Inquiry had called for a full disclosure of all documentation and this had revealed a number of injudicious notes on matters, particularly, from Harvey Hinds. The Inquiry was particularly critical of Harvey Hinds for not having acted sooner. The County Hall machinery had proved to be cumbersome and had been unable to provide a coherent view of what was happening at William Tyndale. Some of the governors were criticized for the way they had conducted themselves: such as instigating a secret petition and feeding information to the press at critical moments when mediation might have been a more effective strategy (see Note 3, Chapter 3). But it was the Authority, rather than the managers, who were criticized for not having set up a framework of school governance which could deal with extreme events, such as those at Tyndale. Some of the reluctance to take on these issues had stemmed from an unwillingness on the part of the ILEA to spell out the power relations between parents, governors and the local authority.

The criticisms within the Auld Report itself, inevitably left many of the 'what if' questions unanswered.

'What if the staff . . . ?'

If only Mr Ellis had responded to the parents . . .

He seemed to resent the fact that parents, who were not 'professional teachers', took it upon themselves to criticise in any way the teaching methods that were being adopted at the school. This reaction stemmed no doubt from the attitude displayed by him in evidence in the Inquiry, that ultimately the teacher must decide how best to teach the children regardless of the views of the parents. (Auld, 1976, para. 256)

If only the teachers had taken a more balanced approach . . .

There is obviously a balance to be struck between too much direction by a teacher, where a child's interest in learning is stifled and too much freedom allowed to the children in which his or her interest in learning is never stimulated . . . On the evidence that I have heard, the Tyndale teachers failed in general to strike the right balance between directions by the teachers and freedom of choice by the the child. (ibid. para. 841)

If only Mr Ellis and his staff had listened to complaints . . .

Miss Hart gave a most disturbing account of the rapid breakdown in the behaviour of the junior school children and its effects on her pupils from the Spring term (1974) onwards — a breakdown which it appeared to her, Mr Ellis and his staff could not or would not recognize and did very little to prevent. She spoke in evidence of Junior School children constantly wandering about the building, in the playground and in the road outside, unsupervised in class hours. She gave many instances of bad behaviour by those children which caused series disruption to the work of the infants school; for example, throwing stones and spitting through the windows of the infants school during class periods; knocking infants' work on window ledges to the floor; throwing articles from upstairs windows into the playground; shouting and rushing about the building during class hours; bullying infants; laughing and swearing at teachers; and abusing the dinner ladies and playground supervisors. (ibid. para. 254)

and had been less intransigent . . .

In persisting with their defiance of the Authority to the extent of going on strike rather than be inspected, the Junior School staff demonstrated how much importance they attached to the inviolability of their 'professional status' and what little thought they had for the children for whose education they were responsible. As a result of their action great harm was caused to the School, and its pupils' education was disrupted quite unnecessarily and in a most damaging manner. (ibid. para. 859)

If only Mrs Walker had acted more professionally . . .

> Largely as a result of Mrs Walker's campaign . . . the atmosphere of
> rumour and counter rumour became all pervading, and Mr Ellis and
> most of his staff spent a disproportionate amount of time on the con-
> spiracies that they believed to be spinning up around them. (ibid.
> para. 372)

'What if the Inner London Education Authority . . . ?'

If only the ILEA had challenged Mrs Walker . . .

> . . . The Authority's administrative machinery failed to deal properly
> with the problems of Mrs Walker . . . (It) presented the problem . . . as
> being essentially an issue between Mr Ellis and the majority of his Staff
> on the one hand, and Mrs Walker on the other. (ibid. para. 409)

If only it had acted more strategically . . .

> The trouble was that the Authority's knowledge was dispersed among
> a number of individuals acting in different capacities and at different
> levels . . . (ibid. para. 586)

If only the Divisional Inspector had given a fuller account of the deteri-
orating conditions and relationships at the school to the Authority . . .

> Mr Rice's report of the 8 July the day before the (parent/teacher
> meeting) is a critical document, because it conditions the attitude of
> the Authority to the school for another six months at least . . . the low
> key way in which the report was expressed . . . appeared to suggest
> that (the problems of the school) could be solved largely by the pro-
> vision of more money and other resources. (ibid. para. 397)

If only Harvey Hinds had acted earlier and more decisively . . .

> Mr Hinds had heard from Mrs Page and others in the Summer of 1974
> of troubles at the Junior School . . . Mr Hinds had no knowledge of the
> extent of the troubles until the Staff wrote to him in September 1974.
> In my view that letter to Mr Hinds was one of the most important indica-
> tions to the Authority in 1974 that the School was in serious trouble.
> It indicated in the clearest terms that the Junior School Staff were in
> conflict with the managers and were questioning the willingness to
> help them of their Divisional Inspector . . . All that Mr Hinds did was
> to decline to intervene in the workings of the local machinery about
> which the Junior School Staff had written to complain. (ibid. para. 885)

Extract from letter from Anne Page to Harvey Hinds, April 1975:

I know that the problem won't go away, and that public involvement will soon be invoked. It may well be time for the (nettle) to be grasped, but surely it should be the Authority which does it, rather than a body of more or less experienced members of the public (the managers)? (ibid. para. 654)

Extract from reply to this letter:

On the subject of William Tyndale, Mr Hinds has asked me to tell you that he does take your point. However, he has consulted with (the leader and deputy leaders of the Authority) on the possible lines of attacking this problem and they are agreed on the present line at the moment. Mr Hinds will of course monitor all the developments closely. (ibid. para. 654)

'What if the school managers . . . ?

If only the school managers had not instigated a 'clandestine' petition . . .

The action taken by (a number of the governors) and others, was thoroughly irresponsible and an act of folly. (ibid. para. 907)

If only they had not used the media in such a high profile way . . .

This proclivity of Mr Tennant (chair of governors) to use Press publicity as a weapon, although he knew it would be generally harmful to the School and its children, was, in my view highly irresponsible, as well as being counter-productive. (ibid. para. 909)

At the end of the Inquiry, the Labour group of politicians attempted to deal with the 'fallout' from Tyndale as quietly as possible. But Anne Page, along with other colleagues, such as Anne Sofer[2] and Ken Livingstone[3] were determined that Harvey Hinds should be called to account for his failure to act. Anne Page argued:

Mr Hinds is censured not only in his capacity as 'Chairman', but also personally. He is censured as severely as any other actor in this drama . . . I think Mr Hinds should like those others blamed in (the) report accept his share . . . of the responsibility for this mess and resign. (Page, 1976)

Although Anne Page and her supporters lost the vote, at a vitriolic meeting of Labour ILEA councillors, *The Times Educational Supplement* ran a front-page headline which read 'Mr Harvey Hinds must go' (TES, 1976a). Harvey Hinds then resigned.

Anne Page's involvement in Tyndale was seen initially by some as 'political orneriness' on her part and an excess of parochialism. It was only as the issues 'hotted' up at Tyndale that other ILEA politicians began to take an interest. Tyndale also represented a political dilemma for the Left. How were they to respond to parent demands? Anne Page recalls returning to County Hall and meeting Ken Livingstone who commented, 'I'm finding it difficult to get a grip on the Left perspective on Tyndale'.

The Impact of Tyndale on Other Teachers

As well as these many unanswerable 'what if?' questions, Tyndale had a major impact on national thinking about the professional role and responsibilities of teachers and headteachers, and on teachers themselves. As the developments unfolded on a national scale, London teachers were drawn into the confrontation, as the Tyndale teachers sought support from their trade union colleagues in the National Union of Teachers (NUT). In the early dates of the dispute, staff had received support and some endorsement from their local colleagues. As the dispute escalated, however, many teachers began to question what was happening at Tyndale. The National Union of Teachers sought to distance itself from events and threatened to discipline the staff if they refused to comply with the ILEA inspection of the school. When interviewed, Fred Jarvis, one-time General Secretary of the NUT, described the Union's attitude to Tyndale in the following terms:

> The Union did not support the teachers because they were a way out group, both in relation to children and in relation to responsibility. Tyndale was not representative of what was happening to schools in London but there was no attempt to put things into perspective. In the long run, William Tyndale was damaging to the teaching profession overall. Politicians used the Tyndale agenda to demonstrate that something needed to be done.

At a key local NUT meeting in Islington in 1975, Tyndale teachers called for support from other Islington teachers in their opposition to the inspection of Tyndale. The motion was lost by 110 votes to 77 (Ellis et al., p. 136). One of the key figures who spoke at that union meeting against the motion of support was Margaret Maden.

Margaret Maden had been drawn into the dispute by her background as a trade unionist and by her proximity to events. In February 1975, she had been appointed as headteacher of Islington Green Comprehensive School. William Tyndale was one of the feeder schools for Islington Green. Staff and governors at Islington Green (who included Anne Page, Maurice Kogan and Robin Mabey, also a school manager at Tyndale) were committed to making comprehensive education work. 'At that time' Margaret Maden recalls, 'it was a great thing to be talking about comprehensive education'. The Islington Green approach was broadly progressive: a very different education model to that offered at Rhodes Boyson's neighbouring Highbury School, with its emphasis on 'the basics' and formal streaming.

Terry Ellis and his colleagues were to later criticize Margaret Maden for her role at the critical union meeting:

> (Margaret Maden) had built up a powerful image as a speaker on education and was often to be seen on television. She spoke with passion about teacher accountability, and claimed the Tyndale staff were shirking their responsibilities to the public. Nothing was said about the accountability of school managers and governors. (Ellis et al., 1976, p. 135)

Margaret Maden herself recalls both the union meeting and events at Tyndale in somewhat different terms:

> There was a nasty feeling in the air (at the meeting) and people were frightened . . . I was struck by the arrogance of the teachers and their refusal to be accountable to anybody. They talked ideological claptrap about working-class kids. The approach they adopted to the reforms in the school was at best unhelpful. It has always been clear to me that if you want to adopt a radical approach to reform in school you have to carry people with you, both parents and governors . . . You need sweat, detail and rigour if you are to develop students' potential. What angered some of us about Tyndale was that there was no structure. It was completely off the wall.

As a headteacher at the time, Margaret Maden had been concerned about the fallout from Tyndale. In her view, the progressive approach adopted at Islington Green had been put in jeopardy by the activities of the Tyndale staff.

How Tyndale Changed Things

The two year power struggle at William Tyndale brought into sharp relief the question 'Who controls schools?' It created demands for a clearer settlement between local authorities, teachers, school governors and parents. It raised issues about teacher professionalism, the autonomy of headteachers, the authority of governors and the rights of parents. Events at Tyndale were as much about the fragmentation of responsibilities between the inspectorate, governors, staff, teachers and parents as a dispute over power. Tyndale also demonstrated conflicting definitions of progressive education and differing interpretations of the needs and aspirations of working-class children.

There is no doubt that the media played a critical role at Tyndale. The teachers were subjected to daily scrutiny and personal abuse in some papers. Among the pupils at William Tyndale was Paul Harter, who later became a film editor. He recalls the school as being a 'wild' one in which the children used to 'chuck milk bottles at each other out of windows'. He also has vivid recollections of the role of the media.

> We used to go journalist baiting, tell them all the lies you could imagine. This was an added bit of fun for us. We made up some great stories. We would find out what they wanted to know and we would make it up for them. There were always one or two around the gate. The news and the BBC were the most exciting. We'd be shouting obscenities.

Children, such as Paul Harter, undoubtedly relished the lime-light and contributed to the press near hysteria. One particular bizarre episode in the school came to epitomize the problems and the growing climate of rumour and counter-rumour which press interest heightened. The controversy centred around a quotation which Mr Haddow had written on the blackboard in his classroom and asked children to write about, or depict in some way. According to Mr Haddow, the quotation which he had used had came from William Blake and read, 'The tigers of wrath are wiser than the horses of instruction'. According to Mrs Chowles and Mrs Walker respectively, Mr Haddow had written, 'The tigers of destruction strong than the horses of instruction,' or 'The tigers of destruction are wiser than the horses of instruction'. The quotation was used as evidence of the way in which Mr Haddow had attempted to indoctrinate children into his own left-wing views (Auld, 1976, paras. 202–4). It later appeared in the *Daily Mail* as 'The smile on the face of the tiger is revolution', a quotation from Chairman Mao (Ellis et al., 1976, p. 22).

Tyndale also brought out of the shadows and into the light of day, issues about the political nature of education and the values embedded in an education system. But whilst the views of Brian Haddow and Terry Ellis were seen as supporting one particular set of political and ideological beliefs, those of Mrs Walker and the Black Paperites were seen as politically neutral. Brian Haddow was later to describe the political debate in the following terms:

> I think all education systems by their very nature of organizing groups of children have a political implication, and that implication is within the organization and values that are transmitted by the system through the school — the rules, the accent on competition as against cooperation, the elitism of achievement and a host of other intricate and subtle things that used to be known as the hidden curriculum. Schools in ILEA are now operating systems that encourage competition, testing and elitism, things which will invigorate a competitive form of capitalism. Whereas we were looking at values that were of a cooperative nature between children, which took positive action on behalf of those children who were coming from disadvantaged circumstances, rather than concentrating resources fully on the high achievers, and that has an overall political implication just as the reverse does. So yes, our education was a political one, but having said that all education is political and has, if you like, indoctrinational implications. (BBC, 1989)

The Auld Report highlighted a number of weaknesses in the system. If a headteacher had a view about teaching methods and the general philosophy of school life which was at odds with the local inspectorate, there were no clear 'yardsticks' to assess the effectiveness of the school's practices. Both local and national politicians at both levels began to see that their job was more than ensuring that schools were provided for.

Tyndale also raised critical issues about the role, powers and responsibilities of the headteacher. The system of school governance at the time was based on assumptions about the professional knowledge and skills of the headteacher. The headteacher offered the main professional judgments and had to be supported in that. Harvey Hinds later described these assumptions about the professional role of the headteacher in the following terms:

> The whole tradition of English education both in the independent and state sectors . . . from Arnold's Rugby onwards has been that you appoint a good headteacher and he runs the show. Now, if he turns out not to be a good headteacher, if he does things wrong, if he does things which parents are dissatisfied with, how do you sack him? . . .

> It was extremely difficult to get rid of a headteacher. He had a kind of freehold which was impossible to break, so you attempted to change his attitude, persuade him to change his methods . . . Nobody felt that we had the right to override in a dictatorial way the professional judgments of the teachers. (BBC, 1989)

Tyndale demonstrated the need for a clearer articulation of what was expected of schools, teachers and headteachers. 'Prior to Tyndale' argues Anne Page, 'no–one asked questions about quality of the curriculum etc and, if you did, you were swatted down'. Issues of school governance were brought to the fore. The Education Authority had powers over school governance which it chose not to exert at that time. It failed to define what the governors 'oversight' of the school meant in practice, despite a number of direct appeals for guidance on this matter, such as that from the chair of governors, Mrs Burnett (reported in Chapter 3).

Tyndale also highlighted that effective school governance is dependent on trust between governors and teachers: an issue which is as critical today as it was in the 1970s and is explored further in Chapter 6. That trust broke down at Tyndale. For school governance to work, headteachers need skill and diplomacy. At Tyndale, professional debate became bitter confrontation, legitimate concerns from parents and governors became interpreted as challenges to the professional integrity of staff.

And there was the issue of intervention, again as critical today as it was then. Why did the Authority appear to be so reluctant to intervene? Why was intervention seen as a last resort? Why did the inspectorate not act in a more authoritative way? Was Tyndale the tip of the iceberg or an aberration? The ILEA was left with some difficult issues to tackle. Peter Newsam, as the administrative leader of the ILEA after Tyndale, was left to tackle the residue of those issues. In his view, the inspectorate had to see itself as part of the main administration, not as a separate entity, an issue which he himself sought to tackle. 'It seems incredible to me' he said, 'that the situation was not identified by the inspectorate'. There were also issues about the degree of openness in the organization and the distribution of decision-making. For Peter Newsam, Tyndale was fundamentally about the nature of political control. To what extent should political control be tightly or loosely exercised? Under very tight control, there is a danger that the creativity and autonomy at the local level which enable schools to flourish will be stifled. Too lose control runs the risk of leaving schools that are 'in trouble' to sort out what may be intractable problems on their own. This is a problem not just of the

1980s, as Peter Newsam suggested but a very real problem of the 1990s, and will be discussed in Chapter 6. The ILEA was caught between the need to democratize and the need to retain accountability.

> The collapse of the junior school was first of all seen as an example of poor primary education within the ILEA. Yet the truth is . . . ILEA's primary schools were improving year by year . . . (and) despite diligent enquiry, the press were unable to find another school like it. More accurately, the incident was seen as an example of the ILEA being indecisive when it should have been firm . . . The point universally missed, however, was *how* this indecisiveness came about. County Hall was inhabited by a number of strong-willed people. Why then this hesitation? The answer is that the individuals concerned were pulled by powerful and contradictory forces. The new policy, vigorously promoted, of openly devolving control to governors and others was in conflict with the older and more authoritarian tradition of secretly directing affairs from County Hall.
>   . . . Robin Auld saw this in legal terms and put the legal point clearly. A public authority can devolve a function but cannot devolve responsibility for its proper exercise . . . The law supports the old authoritarian position . . . (and) the wider problem remains. How is a freedom that can be withdrawn at will to be made genuine, and how is that freedom to be reconciled with the accountability of those who enjoy it? These two problems remain to be tackled in the 1980s. (Newsam, 1981, pp. 4–5)

Undoubtedly, Tyndale also challenged thinking about progressive education. Margaret Maden's concerns about the fallout from Tyndale were well-founded. Despite Peter Newsam's protestation that Tyndale was an aberration, not the tip of an ice-berg, it provided ammunition for those eager to claim evidence that things were adrift in schools. The impact of Tyndale, according to Rhodes Boyson, was that:

> Up to the William Tyndale affair the progressive primary school was running supreme. Colleges of education . . . were turning people about with a sort of liberation, the equivalent in religion to a theology . . . Suddenly ILEA did not like it, and it was a turning point. (BBC, 1989)

Roger Dale sees the outcomes of Tyndale in rather different terms and argues that up to Tyndale, education had considerable autonomy, what he describes as 'licensed autonomy'. 'An implicit licence was granted the education system, which was renewable on the meeting of certain conditions' (Dale, 1989, p. 30). Tyndale was seen as an abuse of the licence. It showed that the picture of a 'tight knit group of politically motivated and irresponsible teachers' was no fantasy (ibid. p. 32). Following Tyndale there was a fundamental shift in control from 'licensed autonomy' to 'regulated autonomy'. Over a period of years following Tyndale and Ruskin, control over the education system became tighter, 'largely through the codification and monitoring of processes and practices previously left to teachers' professional judgement, taken on trust or hallowed by tradition' (ibid. p. 133).

In November 1975, George Cunningham MP, one of the local Islington MPs, rose in the House of Commons on a non too auspicious date, 5 November, to ask the Secretary of State for Education to instigate a special inspection of the school. In his view, Tyndale raised a number of issues about governance which were of profound importance to all those involved in education.

> There is the question of the decline in the frequency and authority of school inspections; there is the means by which disputes of this kind should be resolved; and, finally, there is the part of the Department in the affair.
>
> We have never clearly addressed ourselves in modern times to the question of who should decide matters of curricula and teaching methods in our schools . . . The Department of Education excludes itself from consideration of that subject . . . Local education authorities also tend not to interfere in curriculum matters. The result is that . . . to a great extent, it is left not to the headteacher but to individual teachers.
>
> . . . Coming to the Tyndale affair . . . I want to stress the extent to which the interests of the children are being buried under a mountain of formal procedure. (Hansard, 1975)

Replying for the Government, Joan Lestor, Under Secretary of State for Education and Science, declined to intervene at this stage on the grounds that the ILEA was currently conducting an inquiry and had not as yet requested an inspection from Her Majesty's Inspectorate[4]. Given the extent and nature of the press coverage, most politicians were aware of the issues from late 1975 onwards. There seems little doubt that James Callaghan wanted to differentiate himself and the Labour party from Tyndale and what it represented. Ruskin gave him an opportunity to do just that.

Notes

1   Writing some years after Tyndale in the wake of another public inquiry (to investigate the death of Tyra Henry, a child in the care of Lambeth Social

Services) Stephen Sedley, the QC who defended the Tyndale staff questioned the nature of such judicial hearings. He concluded that an internal inquiry (carried out by external personnel) which limited the rights of each person represented at the hearing to be accompanied by a friend or adviser, might be a more appropriate model, except in the most extreme of circumstances (Lambeth, 1987, pp. 163–4).

2   Anne Sofer was to become chair of the ILEA's Schools Committee and later held the post of Director of Education for Tower Hamlets.

3   Ken Livingstone later became Labour leader of the Greater London Council and a *bête noire* of Mrs Thatcher. He is now a Labour MP and a *bête noire* of Tony Blair. In the wake of Tyndale he campaigned for a reduction in the powers of headteachers, and more parental involvement in schools (Livingstone, 1976).

4   Although this was the first time that Westminster debated these matters, the Tyndale affair had been been drawn to the attention of Government ministers at an earlier stage. Anne Page had spoken to Bryan Davies MP who was then Parliamentary Private Secretary to Fred Mulley, Secretary of State for Education.

Chapter 5

The Ruskin Speech —
Setting a New Agenda?

Mr Christopher Price MP, to the Prime Minister (James Callaghan)
... Does he not agree that it would be a pity if, in the debate that he
has initiated (at Ruskin), we started a movement which made the
teachers in our schools, who are doing a very good job, the scapegoat
for the nation's economic ills? (Hansard, 1976)

The question which remains unanswered about James Callaghan's
Ruskin speech of 1976 is whether it represented a swing towards the
right-wing views of Rhodes Boyson and the 'Black Papers', or whether
it was, as Callaghan himself has maintained, the breaking of new ground
which brought parents into the debate about education and created for
Labour its own distinctive education reform agenda. In re-examining the
speech, I interviewed not only James Callaghan but a number of other
politicians, as well as policy-advisers and educationalists, who were close
to the events of the day, and have drawn on many of those accounts for
this chapter (see Appendix I).

James Callaghan had become Prime Minister in March 1976, following the resignation of Harold Wilson. Before becoming Prime Minister
he had held the posts of Chancellor of the Exchequer, Home Secretary
and Foreign Secretary. The main task facing him as Prime Minister was
to tackle inflation (then running at 21 per cent) but he was also keen
to 'intercede in the cracks' — the spaces between Government departments — and he determined to make his mark in particular policy areas
(Callaghan, 1987, p. 397).

Soon after the leadership election (in which he had defeated Roy
Jenkins, Tony Benn, Michael Foot, Anthony Crosland and Denis Healey)
James Callaghan was given an initial briefing by Bernard Donoughue,
head of the Policy Unit at Number 10 (under both Harold Wilson and
James Callaghan). Three or four possible areas of intervention were suggested and, according to Donoughue, Callaghan determined on education as the priority. 'He didn't really need my briefing on the issue, his
basic instincts were right, that children were not getting a fair deal' —
a point Donoughue also made in his biography (Donoughue, 1987). In

choosing education, Callaghan was able to indulge an old inclination to be Education Minister — one of the few major ministerial portfolios he had not held, although at one stage during his career as Chancellor, Callaghan had asked Harold Wilson whether he could become Secretary of State for Education during a Cabinet reshuffle, a move which Wilson opposed.

During the early months of his administration, James Callaghan met individually with all of his Cabinet ministers to discuss the aims of their particular department. On the 21 May 1976, he met with Fred Mulley, Secretary of State for Education and questioned him about four particular areas:

- Was he satisfied with the basic teaching of the 3 Rs?
- In his view was the curriculum sufficiently relevant and penetrating for older children in comprehensive schools?
- How did the examination system shape up as a test of achievement?
- What was available for the further education of sixteen to nineteen year olds? (Callaghan, 1987, p. 469)

Fred Mulley was asked to prepare a memorandum on these matters by early July 1976. According to Margaret Beckett MP, who was a Junior Education Minister at the time, Fred Mulley had been pleasantly surprised by Callaghan's interest in education. Callaghan had emphasized standards and the importance of not letting working-class people down. Education was their right and a Labour Government would give it a high priority.

As James Callaghan pondered the education issues in the summer of 1976, the press was full of stories about the William Tyndale affair. It had begun in 1974 and had first hit the headlines in 1975, with almost daily national coverage from October 1975, to February 1976 (the period of the Public Inquiry about the school). For all of this period, Callaghan was busy being Foreign Secretary, but Tyndale became the centre of national media attention again in July 1976, with the publication of the findings of the Inquiry, which castigated most of those involved, particularly the teachers. The July 1976 newspaper headlines which James Callaghan must have pondered as he prepared for Ruskin included the following:

Save Our Children (Sunday Telegraph)

The Victims: It has taken over two years to discover what every parent knew by instinct from the outset: William Tyndale Junior School was a shambles (The Sun)

Parents Must Have More Say in Schools (Evening News)

Rate Payers Lose Again (Evening News)

The Classroom Despots (Evening Standard)

The Tragedy of William Tyndale (Observer)

How to Control the Teachers (Sunday Times)

Mulley Steps in at Troubled School (Daily Mail)

ILEA Chief Quits in Tyndale Row (Sun)

Events at Tyndale consolidated Callaghan's apprehensions about education and nourished many of his own long-held beliefs. It focused attention on 'irresponsible teachers' and raised issues about teacher professionalism, the control of schools and the needs and aspirations of working-class children. It became a national press scandal and un-doubtedly, was a catalyst for change. According to Anne Page, Callaghan had wanted to differentiate himself and the Labour Party from Tyndale and what it represented, a view which Callaghan himself endorsed when I questioned him about Tyndale in 1996, 'I was determined that the Tories were not going to line us up with Tyndale . . . and every idiotic teacher who was sympathetic to the Labour Party', he stated.

The Tyndale spotlight turned a sharp beam on a group of teachers who appeared to think that preparing young people for work was pandering to the state. Such views were a deep anathema to James Callaghan, who was concerned about issues of privilege, and the lack of access and opportunities for working-class people. His own personal com-mitment to education and his perception that working-class parents were concerned about schools, not least issues of discipline, reinforced his determination to initiate a debate about education and to open up the 'Secret Garden' of curriculum and the professional world of the teacher. During the course of my interview with Callaghan, he explained his views on education and the background to the Ruskin speech.

> I was concerned with what was being said to me in the constituency about literacy and numeracy, not exactly in those terms but people were talking to me about those things. Some parents were expressing

disquiet as to whether their children were being taught or not, because of the child-centred approach . . .

There was a general feeling around that there was something not
quite right (about schools). If the parents were unhappy and dissatis-
fied, it seemed to me that we ought to look at this. This met with a lot
of resentment and created such a furore that I should dare to talk about
those things but in fact it was a thing that had gone on for years . . .

There was a feeling of dissatisfaction. The 1944 settlement seemed
to be getting frayed at the edges, particularly by the activity of the
unions. The teachers seemed to be demanding more and of course
they got what they wanted (the Houghton Pay Award) but still did not
seem to be happy . . .

The Tyndale school was rattling on getting a lot of publicity and
that wasn't doing the teaching profession any good . . . The government could not escape its responsibility. I was also talking to the CBI
about those battles and they were complaining about the quality of the
school. They always do and still are. I spoke with Bernard Donoughue
as I was looking for themes which I could take up as Prime Minister.
I thought it would be nice for me to do something. The fun of being
Prime Minister is being able to intervene whenever you wish.

Bernard Donoughue's argument was that the education system of
the day reinforced under-privilege, restricting opportunities for working-
class children. He was highly critical of the education experience of his
own children in the state school system in Islington (close to William
Tyndale) and of the ways in which, in his view, education had been
taken over by middle-class ideologues.

Ruskin was based on my instinctive and basic belief that education
was one of the most important issues in society. In any case, the
Government had to get the economy right, but education was what
really mattered. All this was being ruined by a bunch of middle-class
ideologues who did not themselves have a proper experience of state
education. Their prejudices were at the expense of working-class children. There was clear evidence that working-class parents and children wanted education and what they wanted was not the same as the
middle-class Labour people from Islington, the trendy lecturers from
higher education who wanted education at the expense of working-
class kids. Jim and I talked about this. Whenever I heard those people
talk I got very angry . . . Their thinking was based on *Guardian* style
ideologies and prejudices.

In Bernard Donoughue's view of events, the NUT seemed to support
the vested interests of particular groups of teachers and focused on the

needs of teachers to the exclusion of children and parents. 'The NUT teachers represented the worst side of the teaching profession and diminished the role of the traditional dedicated teacher'[1].

But was there a major problem in education? There were conflicting views in 1976 about how effectively education was structured and whether children were being well served or not[2]. A key source of information at the time was what came to be known as 'The Yellow Book', a document commissioned by James Callaghan which gave the views of the then Department of Education and Science and Her Majesty's Inspectorate on the 'health' of the education system. How far was Tyndale an aberration, or did it reflect what was happening in many schools throughout the country? 'The Yellow Book' was a classified document and I was not able to gain access to a copy; but a number of interviewees had been privy to its contents and one described it to me in the following terms:

> One of the things you don't hear about is what 'The Yellow Book' contained. Overall it was very positive, it recognized the achievements of education, such as the fact that schools had made a reality of secondary education for all, and that educational achievement had been mobilized. There had been a massive and successful rebuilding and restructuring programme after the war. 'The Yellow Book' said to the Prime Minister that things are not as bad as you thought, although there obviously are issues that need pushing forward. For example, perhaps the Schools Council needed greater clarity. There are also issues in relation to preparation for work.
>
> Teachers were not layabouts but the problem was that they did not necessarily understand the standards . . . to be achieved by children. 'The Yellow Book' definitely refuted the notion, however, that inspection was the way forward . . . The problem about inspection is that politicians think that the act of inspection itself will make a difference. It will only make a difference if it has an impact on what teachers think about their work. It is only if they accept the evidence of inspection that it is possible to have improvement.

The education unions also had strong, if conflicting, views about the state of education. Fred Jarvis from the NUT was unconvinced that there were major problems about standards.

> I welcome the statement made by the Prime Minister that education is more important than ever because of the kind of world we are living in, and I am certainly not afraid of a debate on the kind of education we are going to provide for the nation's children . . . It is a pity that the Prime Minister didn't acknowledge that the Department of Education

stated in the summer that many more children are today leaving schools with qualifications than at any other time in our history. That would have been a more balanced appraisal of what is going on. (ITN, 1976)

Terry Casey from the National Association of Schoolmasters had a very different perspective. In his view, the education system was being undermined by the liberal philosophies of the day.

We welcome the Prime Minister's interest and concern. He is joining us because for 20 or 30 years we have been expressing concern that the education service is not being as effective as it might be because of the intervention of rather crackpot theorists who seek to suborn and seduce teachers from their proper responsibility for standards . . . (BBC, 1976)

Those people responsible for this sorry state of affairs were the DES itself and their inspectors, and local authority advisers. According to Terry Casey, they had 'played a part in trading these gimmicks on schools' and James Callaghan offered a sense of new realism.

The Ruskin Speech: A 'Clarion Call' to What?

Ruskin was undoubtedly a very personal affair for James Callaghan which sprang from his own commitment to education, as he explained:

Education was a pearl beyond price to the Labour Movement, it was a way, if you like, where we could escape from our background. I went to school but to go to a university was unthinkable, so education and Ruskin meant a lot to my generation.

He regretted not having had the opportunity to go to university and saw education as the vehicle which would open opportunities for working-class children. The invitation from an old friend, Billy Hughes (Principal of Ruskin College and one time Labour MP), to lay a Foundation Stone for an extension of the College, provided the ideal opportunity for him to make a speech — and for intervention on education[3].

In his October 1976 speech, James Callaghan spoke about parental concerns about teaching methods. 'There is the unease felt by parents about the new informal methods of teaching which seem to produce excellent results when they are in well-qualified hands but are much more dubious in their effects when they are not'. He pointed to a number of areas of national concern, such as the low standards of numeracy for school leavers; the high proportion of girls abandoning science at an early age; vacancies in science and technology courses; and the unwillingness of university/polytechnic graduates to join industry. He argued for the setting of national standards; monitoring of increasingly scarce resources; and a core curriculum of basic knowledge. It was vitally important that relationships between schools and industry were improved. 'The goals of education from nursery education to adult education are clear enough' he contended, 'they are to to equip children to the best of their ability for a lively constructive place in society and also to fit them to do a job of work. Not one or the other but both'. He claimed that his speech was not made as a 'clarion call to Black Paper prejudices', but as a way of airing concerns and shortcomings in the system so that they could be righted (Callaghan, 1976).

Looking at the speech some two decades later, the themes and issues look familiar — the everyday language and aspirations of politicians — and it is difficult to understand why the speech caused such a stir at the time. But in 1976, Ruskin appeared to question many Labour assumptions and was seen by some as an attack on teacher supremacy. Chris Price certainly thought so, as is shown in the following exchange in the House of Commons on 19 October, the day after the speech.

Mr Christopher Price: Reverting to my Right Hon Friend's speech yesterday when he suggested that our education system provided part of the cure for our economic ills, is he aware that some Government supporters have considerable concern and apprehension that we load on to our schools too much of an exclusively economic role? Does he not agree that it would be a pity if, in the debate that he has initiated, we started a movement which made the teachers in our schools, who are doing a very good job, the scapegoat for the nation's economic ills?

The Prime Minister: Nothing that I have said so far should lead to that conclusion. I have pointed out some worrying factors, namely the large number of vacancies — I am told 30,000 or so — for scientific and technical students in our universities and polytechnics. This is a very serious matter which the nation should consider. I have pointed out the lack of co-ordination that seems to exist between industry and education. I have asked that there should be a better link between the two, and I shall try to do that. But I do not put anyone in the dock on this. We, as a nation, are too fond of trying to find scapegoats and of putting people in the dock. We have to discover what is wrong and try to work towards putting it right. (Hansard, 1976)

James Callaghan had intended to raise questions about teachers and teaching but neither at the time, nor subsequently, did he see Ruskin as having 'kicked off' a scape-goating process as Chris Price had. He argued that for him, an essential part of Ruskin was about stimulating a debate about the relationship between industry and education, as well as the objectives and outcomes of education and training. In response to a question posed to him in Parliament during an economic debate also held on the 19 October, he outlined this theme.

> *The Prime Minister:* I am not saying that the responsibility (for the economy) rests wholly on one side. There are certainly employers who feel that the education system is not producing people with the basic knowledge that they need when they are recruited. On the other hand, some parts of the education service feel that employers could do more to bring their requirements to the notice of the education service. I think I have succeeded in my objective of starting a debate — indeed, it started before I ever said one word, thanks, I think, to some infighting that went on somewhere, which I do not know much about. I hope that the discussions will continue. I am now considering ways that I can focus them on some of these issues. (ibid. 1976)

Despite this public focus on the relationship between industry and education, Callaghan admitted privately at that time that he had challenged the received wisdom of education professionals. Roy Hattersley, whose wife Molly was a headteacher (and later became a senior administrator in the Inner London Education Authority), recalled a conversation outside the Cabinet room, 'I remember him (Callaghan) saying to me as we were waiting to go into Cabinet "Molly won't like it". And she didn't'.

Although informal exchanges took place outside Cabinet about the Ruskin speech, it was not a topic for debate within the Cabinet itself. Tony Benn was another Cabinet minister whose wife (Caroline) was deeply involved in education issues. He recalls Shirley Williams passing him a note in Cabinet on the 14 October, four days before the Ruskin speech, which read 'Tony, no question of any change in emphasis on comprehensives. It's mainly on maths, why not enough kids are doing engineering, etc. A bit about standards. Curriculum will be the main row' (Benn, 1989, p. 626). Tony Benn's interest in education drove him to try (unsuccessfully) to acquire a copy of 'The Yellow Book'; a document which was leaked ahead of the Ruskin speech to *The Times Education Supplement.* Tony Benn's view of the impact of the speech was that:

(Ruskin) was most damaging to the cause of comprehensive education. After years of inactive Education Secretaries, we now have in Shirley Williams a right-wing one working with a Prime Minister who has allowed himself to be briefed by Department of Education officials who themselves don't use the state system and are deeply hostile to it. (ibid. p. 627)

At a Trades Union Council–Labour Party meeting soon after Ruskin, Tony Benn recalls the debate continuing. Callaghan spoke of the need for a core curriculum. Tony Benn welcomed the debate about education which Ruskin had begun, but reiterated his view that the speech itself represented a major attack on comprehensive education. Shirley Williams, also present at the meeting, warned against a backlash but argued that there were genuine concerns about teaching methods and the ways in which education for the 16–19 age group was organized (ibid. p. 629).

Although Tony Benn referred to the Ruskin speech in his memoirs, other senior Cabinet members of the time did not. Despite Tony Crosland's earlier interest and involvement in education in the first Wilson Government (see Chapter 2), Susan Crosland's biography of her husband does not mention the Ruskin speech (Crosland, 1982). When I interviewed David Lipsey, political adviser to Tony Crosland in 1976, he was not surprised that the events of Ruskin had gone unrecalled. At the time, Tony Crosland had been engrossed in his role as Foreign Secretary.

For Denis Healey and Barbara Castle, the pressing issue of the time was the sterling crisis and the IMF (Healey, 1989; Castle, 1993). Particular aspects of that drama had come to a head in the early autumn of 1976 (some two weeks before the Ruskin speech) at the Labour Party Conference at Blackpool. Barbara Castle recalls arriving at Blackpool to be faced with press accounts of Denis Healey's dramatic turn around at Heathrow. (He had been due to fly to Hong Kong for a meeting of Commonwealth Foreign Ministers but had abandoned his flight plans and had dashed back to London for talks about the 'crumbling' pound.) Later during that week, Healey had come to the Party Conference announcing that he had 'come from the battle front' and had agreed to apply to the IMF for credit (Castle, 1993, p. 499). The economic and political news throughout the autumn of 1976 was dominated, therefore, by negotiations about the extent and nature of the IMF loan which would support the British economy, and the size of the cuts package demanded by the IMF as one of the conditions for the loan.

Given the political and economic context, one of the questions which I inevitably explored with interviewees was the extent to which the Ruskin speech had been a smokescreen: a diversion from the main economic agenda. There seems to be no evidence to suggest (from either Callaghan's supporters or detractors) that there had been a calculated strategy to divert attention from the crisis. The Ruskin initiative was undoubtedly driven by Callaghan's abiding passion for the education of working-class children. However, given the IMF context and the growing pressures on the Callaghan Government, as Bernard Donoughue said: in his interview with me.

> When ever a front bench team thinks its losing it, they want to come up with a policy that grabs the nation. Given the Ruskin invitation and Jim's passion for education we obviously asked what can we make of it? How could we make connections and move the debate on?

Chance undoubtedly played its part in events.

Although the Ruskin speech was not a tactical diversion, it does seem, however, to have been one of the many occasions in which the political 'spin doctors' were active. Tom McCaffery (head of the Number 10 Press Office) and Bernard Donoughue met on a number of occasions to decide on a fresh approach. They briefed journalists systematically and Donoughue recalls having spoken to more journalists on the issues about Ruskin than on any other issue. Donoughue was convinced, as Callaghan, that the only way to deal with the vested interests of educational professionals was to stimulate a public debate. According to Bernard Donoughue, Shirley Williams had wanted to hold the debate behind closed doors with the professional community. She had not been opposed to the general thrust of Ruskin but had been concerned about how it would be received. She had not wanted to be left in the lurch if she found that the Prime Minister had changed his position. 'In this', Bernard Donoughue told me, 'she grossly underestimated Jim. He was very determined about the issue'.

Given this attention to the nature of the public debate, the speech itself was no surprise to the media which had been well prepared for a significant speech by the Prime Minister on education. Key elements of the debate had been leaked to *The Times Educational Supplement* (TES) in advance of the speech. Nevertheless, the TES reacted to the speech in a front page editorial in the following terms:

> He (the Prime Minister) has gathered his Black Paper cloak around him. He has trotted out cliches from the CBI about the shortcomings of young workers. He has dodged the question of whether he thinks standards are rising or falling . . . He has whistled up weasel words to

exploit popular prejudice . . . He has sought to divert popular indigna-
tion from . . . his own management of the economy to the teachers'
management of the curriculum. (TES, 1976b)

The Times viewed it as a 'shade disappointing' and suggested
that it was somewhat 'otiose' for the Prime Minister to call for a debate
when 'the buzz of debate about education is incessant and stupefying'.
The editorial view was that the debate heralded a 'reverse swing of the
education pendulum' which suited the 'leanness and meanness of the
times . . . very different from the free-wheeling, expansionist enthusiasms
which inspired the world of education in the big-spending years of
middle and late sixties' (Times, 1976).

Ruskin undoubtedly represented a shift in thinking about education and was certainly a defining moment[4]. It raised questions about
curriculum control and suggested that teachers were not the only legitimate group to have an interest in education. As *The Times* suggested,
it reflected the 'leanness and meanness' of the day but also signalled
the end of the belief in education as a 'good' which simply required
increased investment. It raised issues of accountability and control and
echoed some of the concerns in the Black Papers. In attempting to move
that debate into the centre ground, it represented for Labour a shift to
the Right in thinking about education. Interviewed in 1996, Rhodes
Boyson described Ruskin as, 'politically, a very good speech. I could
have gone along with that'.

The Impetus for the Speech

When I talked to a number of politicians and officials of the day about
the genesis of the speech and Callaghan's motivation in making it,
two different themes emerged. To some, Callaghan had a 'chip' on his
shoulder about his own lack of formal education. He was a deeply conservative politician who, as Home Secretary, had been shocked at the
behaviour of students involved in the 1968 students' revolts. To others,
including several of those closest to him, Callaghan was an astute politician with a passion for education, who sensed that the public mood
had shifted in a way which supported his own gut instincts. His background in the unions had shaped many of his views about education,
including a strong commitment to apprenticeships. Margaret Beckett
saw Callaghan and Ruskin in those terms:

It is important to remember that Callaghan was a trade union official.
For him education was the key. It was part of an important channel of

communication. He talked about 'education for life' and in this he was very much ahead of his field. He wanted to ensure that there were close links between education and industry.

Bernard Donoughue endorsed Callaghan's deep and personal commitment to the issues. 'In my view, the political judgement of Callaghan on this matter was excellent. Jim's personal commitment was the single most important issue in relation to Ruskin'. Elizabeth Hartley-Brewer (née Arnott), who worked in the Number 10 Policy Unit with Bernard Donoughue and had been closely involved in drafting the speech, described Callaghan as 'a traditionalist' who was very committed to education having come up the hard way and 'was suspicious of high flown ideology'.

Those who thought Callaghan had a 'chip' on his shoulder about his own lack of formal education gave accounts of conversations (at dinner for example) in which Callaghan questioned the guests about who had got a 'first' or a 'second' from Oxbridge. Critics perceived Callaghan as a deeply conservative man whose conservativism had been reinforced by his period as Home Secretary during the late 1960s. According to this analysis, Callaghan's target was 'trendy' teachers and what he aimed to do, and succeeded in doing, was to move schools in a different, more traditional direction, to the right.

Chris Price who had became Parliamentary Private Secretary to Fred Mulley in the summer of 1975, a post which he held for just over a year, traced the roots of Ruskin back to Callaghan's personal beliefs. 'Callaghan is a deeply conservative Methodist, very concerned about propriety and behaviour and strongly influenced by Wesleyan traditions and the events of the 1960s'. In Price's view, 1968 and the student revolts caused a schism within the Labour Party. Politicians, such as Tony Crosland and Harold Wilson, had very much welcomed the student 'sit ins' and Wilson, in particular, had been overjoyed at the upheavals, feeling that he had unleashed that radical streak through his own policies. Ted Short and James Callaghan, however, had been deeply affronted at the student revolts and sympathized with aspects of the Black Papers. The issues of 1968 ('the clash that never came out in the Labour Party') did not surface because in 1970 Labour lost the General Election[5].

These differing views about Callaghan may not be as contradictory as they first appear and Denis Healey's account of Callaghan's premiership appears to endorse both perceptions. In his view, Callaghan was for the most part 'the best of Britain's postwar prime ministers after Attlee' (Healey, 1989, p. 447). Callaghan had 'none of the middle-class socialist's illusions about how working-class people think', and was determined to give working-class people 'a fairer share of wealth and opportunity' (ibid. p. 448). It was on these grounds that Callaghan had been bitterly opposed to Harold Wilson's proposal in 1968 to postpone the raising of the school-leaving age for two years because of the cost.

At the same time, however, Healey also suggested that Callaghan had not been a very distinguished Chancellor and in Opposition had been seen as opportunistic. On social issues Callaghan was 'as conservative as the trade union movement which provided his political base' (op. cit). Healey cites, as examples of Callaghan's innate conservatism, his opposition, as Prime Minister, to amending the Official Secrets Act and his comments in 1966 about a ban on supplying arms to South Africa, which had sparked off a crisis at the time (ibid. p. 334). His views about Callaghan's perceptions of the 1960s during his period as Home Secretary are not dissimilar to those of Chris Price. 'Many of the new freedoms demanded by the student intellectuals of the sixties found him perplexed and even innocent' (ibid. p. 448).

In the field of social policy, both Denis Healey and Barbara Castle refer to Callaghan's decision to oppose the introduction of Child Benefit, on the basis that it would upset male voters, although in somewhat different terms. Healey comments, 'It was (Callaghan) who first realized that the Child Benefit, which had figured so long in Labour Party programmes, might cost us male votes because it would mean a switch from the wallet to handbag; it would be paid to the wife at the cost of withdrawing a tax allowance from the husband' (op. cit.). Barbara Castle remarks:

> There was no attempt to argue that (the indefinite postponement of Child Benefit) was being done on economic grounds. Jim Callaghan openly admitted that he had done this to assuage the sensitivities of the male wage-earner, who would find his take-home pay reduced in order to switch the money to his wife. The unions, he claimed, would never accept such a switch at a time when we were urging pay restraint. Jim was a deeply conventional and pragmatic man, who never understood the idealistic values of the left. Decency, yes. Dreaming, no. (Castle, 1993, p. 492)

Callaghan's perceptions about the roots of the problems confronting education seem, therefore, to have been driven by two sets of deeply-held beliefs. The first stemmed from a belief in the rights of working-class children to have access to opportunities in education. The second stemmed from an innate conservatism which opposed radical change to the social order. Both sets of beliefs found expression in the Ruskin speech. The economic context in which the speech took place was one

of retrenchment, in which the ability of the education system to contribute to economic prosperity was increasingly being challenged.

The Ruskin Legacy

Some fifteen years after Ruskin, at a special conference to mark the
event, James Callaghan recalled Ruskin in the following terms:

> Of all the countless speeches I have delivered in a long political life,
> the Ruskin speech is the one that is best remembered . . . It attracted
> wide publicity . . . because it touched a sensitive spot among parents
> and employers . . . By some of the educational elite it was thought to
> be an unseemly intrusion of the Prime Minister to poke his nose into
> educational matters and stir up trouble on matters best left to those
> who know most . . . The effect at the time was like a stone dislodged
> by the mountaineer's foot which, rolling down the mountain side, pre-
> cipitates an avalanche. Since then, the debate on aims and methods,
> structure and content has hardly stopped . . . (Callaghan, 1992, p. 9)

Reflecting on the speech some twenty years on, Callaghan commented
to me:

> I have re-read the speech. I think its rather gentle and I think it has
> been my political philosophy all the way through. You can do more
> things by persuasion, just as I wanted the trade unions to do but
> failed. That's always been my reasoning to try a different approach . . . I
> did not want to antagonize the teachers, I recognized their respons-
> ibilities. I did think that recruitment of teachers to some extent in the
> 60s had gone adrift. I was not impressed with what was emerging in
> some areas. On the other hand, you had that whole core of experi-
> enced teachers who were the product of the 40s and the 50s.

Looking back, it is difficult to assess how far Ruskin fed off the Black
Papers, or fed into them. The Black Papers were certainly an important
part of the context: a sustained and systematic attack on the perceived
failure of state education. According to Tessa Blackstone, however, (at
the time a member of the Central Policy Review Staff [CPRS] and later
Baroness Blackstone and Minister of State for Education) Ruskin was
not driven by the Black Papers[6]. The events of Tyndale were influential
and members of the CPRS, who advised the Prime Minister on education matters, were aware of emerging criticisms about teaching methods
(see Chapter 2). In Blackstone's view, the significance of Ruskin was to

suggest that there was a need for a common curriculum and for more central government control and input on education. On a personal level, Blackstone maintained that Callaghan was a much more reflective person than people gave him credit for. One of his strengths was that he was able to pick up on a range of underlying concerns: parental worries about the ways in which schools were being controlled and managed; emerging concerns that the influence of trade union leaders extended far beyond their legitimate brief; and that the professional agenda had been taken over by teachers. 'Some of those in positions of power in education held ideological views that were very far removed from everyday realities and out of tune with parents'.

Callaghan's Ruskin speech has been described by some as a turning point in Labour thinking about education. According to Bernard Donoughue, Ruskin served to challenge a range of vested interests, including the Department of Education and Science and the National Union of Teachers. Bernard Donoughue had strong and influential opinions about the role of teacher unions and the NUT in particular. He also argued that until the Ruskin speech the Labour Party had largely ignored the views of parents and that policy-making within the Labour Party was dominated by unrepresentative groups who themselves were rarely parents.

The significance of Ruskin are that it raised questions about curriculum control and suggested that teachers were not the only legitimate group to have an interest in the curriculum. It reflected a view that issues such as standards were not just part of the Conservative agenda, but were the legitimate concerns of people within the Labour Party. It raised questions about the use of resources and brought to the fore a current of unease which some argued had been prevalent for a number of years.

Ruskin undoubtedly signalled a political change in that national Government indicated that it wished to set policy objectives for education and to apply criteria to the public sector. In this way it challenged professional control and autonomy and the authority of teachers' unions. Some have argued that the significance of the speech lies in the fact that it was the first time that a Prime Minister had tried to set the agenda for education, something which is now taken for granted. Both John Major and Tony Blair have attempted to put their stamp on education. Others have challenged this view, pointing out that both Gladstone and Disraeli were deeply involved in education and that Harold Wilson had demonstrated a personal commitment through the establishment of the Open University (as a way of opening out access to education for the working-classes) and through the raising of the school leaving age.

Views about Ruskin — its genesis and impact — will no doubt remain mixed. The only certainty today is that the last Labour Prime Minister to have held all the great Ministerial Offices of State is already best remembered for the contribution he made in a policy area, education, for which he never held direct ministerial responsibility.

Notes

1 He suggested to me that his views had been influenced by the experience of his wife who had been a school inspector and had also worked for a short time at the headquarters of the NUT.

2 Some concerns about education emerged during the 'Roadshows' which followed on from Ruskin as part of the 'Great Debate'. The 'Roadshows' — which took place throughout the country — were led by Shirley Williams, who had taken over from Fred Mulley as Secretary of State for Education in the summer of 1976, and her ministerial team which included Margaret Beckett.

3 Ruskin College, Oxford was set up by the Trade Union and Labour Movement as a college which would provide educational opportunities for trade union and Labour activists. It was named after John Ruskin the nineteenth century philosopher and educationalist.

4 Roger Dale has argued that Jim Callaghan's Ruskin speech and the series of events which surrounded it (including the 'Yellow Book', the 'Great Debate', and the Green Paper on Education in 1977) signified a departure from the principles in the 1944 Act. In his view, Ruskin was a 'watershed in the post-war history of education' because the settlement enshrined in the 1944 Act was showing signs of strain and breakdown (Dale, 1989, p. 105).

5 Callaghan's own biography, which includes his period as Home Secretary in 1968, gives little indication of his view of events, although it recounts the tactics adopted to avoid violence at a march and demonstration against the Vietnam War (Callaghan, 1987).

6 The Central Policy Review Staff (CPRS) at Number 10 was known as 'the Think Tank'. It had originally been set up by Ted Heath to offer advice to ministers on future policy directions and was influential throughout the 1970s. It was abolished by Margaret Thatcher in 1983 (Blackstone and Plowden, 1990).

Chapter 6

Thatcher's Legacy: Blair's New World

. . . Whether educational changes are polity-directed through peaceful manipulation or are the products of explosion followed by panic legislation, they constitute a distinctive 'stop-go' pattern. Periods of stasis are punctuated by legislative reforms and change advances by jerks rather than by accretion or modifications. In all cases, universal reforms fail to satisfy, they are followed by a period in which grievances build up and finally result in another universal reform, the cycle repeating indefinitely. Margaret Archer (1979, p. 17)

The Thatcher Revolution

Education is shaped by a range of factors. These include our own national expectations, the efforts of national and local government, as well as international and global trends and influences. Both Tyndale and Ruskin in their different ways have helped shape our thinking about education and our expectations about schools. The legacies of Tyndale and Ruskin remain in current debates about who rules schools; about whether teachers teach children or impart their knowledge to them; and about whether a government is getting a worthwhile return for its investments in education. This chapter takes the story forward from the 1970s and explores the Thatcher legacy: the metamorphosis of Margaret Thatcher from Secretary of State for Education, to Leader of the Conservative Party (following the election defeat of Ted Heath in 1974), and finally, in 1979, to Prime Minister. It finishes in 1997, with the election of a Labour Government headed by Tony Blair.

I was teaching in 1979, when Margaret Thatcher first came to power, introduced her particular brand of Conservatism, and created new myths about leadership. Since 1979 and the election of that first Thatcher Government, a succession of Conservative administrations have introduced a series of radical changes aimed at creating a more market-orientated public sector, characterized by choice and competition, and made more accountable through a range of performance mechanisms. A major inspiration for Thatcher was the free-market ideologue, Frederick Hayek, who endorsed as his basic tenet what he described as 'the catallaxy: the spontaneous relations of free market exchange between individuals' (Wainwright, 1994, p. 42). In *The Road to Serfdom*, his most popular polemic against socialism (which Secretary of State for Education Keith Joseph made compulsory reading for his civil servants), Hayek argued against any form of state intervention: either by the command economies of communist states, or by Keynesian or moderate social democratic governments (Hayek, 1991). Hayek inspired Thatcher to believe that by withdrawing the state from the economy, she had released, as she herself described it, 'the spirit of enterprise' (Wainwright, 1994, p. 62).

In those early days of Thatcher Government, educational policy was not a major preoccupation and was discussed little at Cabinet level (Wapshott and Brock, 1983, p. 104). However, the political, economic and ideological influences which later combined to alter the educational landscape were at play. Thatcher's first appointment to the position of Secretary of State for Education was Mark Carlisle who offered a strong critique of state education (although one not dissimilar to that of Labour Prime Minister, James Callaghan, in his Ruskin speech). But he limited the influence of the emergent radical right, and reasserted the 'One Nation Philosophy' of his Conservative predecessors (Knight, 1990, p. 137).

During Keith Joseph's tenure as Secretary of State (from 1981 to 1986), the battle for supremacy within the Conservative Party raged between the decentralizers, who aimed to maximize parental choice, and the centralizers, the One Nation Tories who aimed to maximize pupil performance (ibid. pp. 156–8). Keith Joseph ultimately sided with the One Nation Tories. Excellence, differentiation, relevance, fitness for purpose and value for money were his educational goals. The language of choice and competition had yet to emerge (Riley, 1994a).

But emerge it did. Throughout the 1980s, central government and local government were locked in a perpetual poker game. When the Government 'upped the ante' there were casualties, such as the GLC. Partly through Keith Joseph's intervention, the Inner London Education Authority (ILEA) was spared, and a directly elected ILEA created. In 1986, I became one of the first, and last, of those ILEA elected councillors.

My time as an ILEA member coincided with the Conservatives' third administration. It was during this period that Kenneth Baker launched the Enterprise Culture on a wary education world. I well remember the frantic consultation exercise during the summer of 1987, which paved the way for the introduction of the 1988 Act. This was followed in the autumn by the amendment to abolish the ILEA which was introduced during a late night sitting of a committee stage of the Bill by Michael

Heseltine MP, in a move designed to appease the radical right. Norman Tebbit MP described the shift which the 1988 Act was intended to create in the following terms:

> The Bill extends choice and responsibility. Some will choose badly, or irresponsibly, but that cannot be used to deny choice and responsibility to the great majority. (Hansard, 1987)

The wheel had turned full circle from the post war consensus. All politicians now saw it as their business to define educational objectives. It was for teachers to deliver the outcomes. The 1988 Act, reinforced by subsequent legislation, created a new language and set of expectations about competition and diversity, accountability and choice, and the promotion of individual rights. In the new education market, a heavily prescribed national agenda co-existed uneasily with increased devolution of powers to schools and governing bodies.

It is important not to underestimate both the nature of the changes over the last twenty years, and the extent to which they have impacted on our views about the nature of society, and the roles of individuals within that society. Margaret Thatcher herself has been a dominating influence on events. Her political attitudes and brand of Conservative thinking — what came to be known as 'Thatcherism' — have pervaded many areas, including education. Margaret Thatcher shared with Jim Callaghan an uncanny ability to identify with the changing mood of the times. In the mid-1970s, Callaghan sensed the growing unease about state education, the frustrations of working-class parents and the aspirations of those who saw education as the route upwards. In the 1980s, Margaret Thatcher capitalized on the growing lack of deference, the new assertion of individual rights. People were simply no longer prepared 'to be told', 'to put up with'.

Many people who do not support her policies have a sneaking admiration for Thatcher's challenge to the notions of deference, but the problem about Margaret Thatcher's assertion of individual rights was that it encouraged an acquisitive culture which lacked community responsibility. In challenging deference, Margaret Thatcher freed parents to question the legitimacy of those education professionals who had conceived education as the sole responsibility of teachers and officials, and schools as places in which parents were at best tolerated. But she failed to replace deference with new modes of respect: the pupil and parent for the teacher, and the teacher for the pupil and the parent. Instead of creating a climate of professional responsibility and mutuality between professionals and parents, Margaret Thatcher created a surveillance culture and an acquisitive and individualistic, rights-based notion of citizenship. The State should, as far as it could, leave people as free as possible to pursue their interests through market choices. Market mechanisms would lead not only to efficiency but also to freedom and democracy (Walsh, 1991).

Over the last twenty years, our thinking about what education is, who decides what it is, who gets it and how, has undergone a transformation. The reform agenda has been heavily influenced by prevailing economic theories which emphasize choice, economy and efficiency. Higher education has changed from a minority experience to a mass commodity. The notion of education as a public good, freely available to all those who require it, has been brought into question by the gradual erosion of student grants and the introduction of loans, tuition fees, and the prospect of 'top-up' fees to elite institutions (see Note 7). The predominantly public monopoly of education has been challenged by the creation of market opportunities for private providers. Education has become the business of the state in very specific ways, but individuals (pupils and their parents) are increasingly being held responsible for their own engagement in education. Parents have rights but they also have responsibilities.

The impact of a rights-based notion of citizenship has, with some inevitability in recent years, led to a number of conflicts within the field education. At Manton School in Nottinghamshire, for example, the determination of one set of parents to assert their rights about their child's education clashed with the assertions of teachers to maintain their rights not to teach difficult children (see Chapter 7). The clash was an indication of the frustrations of parents, pupils and teachers and of major problems in the system. It demonstrated the need for a rethinking of the responsibilities of the various players (governors, headteachers, LEAs and national government), as well as the need for a mediation framework at the local level.

A rights-based notion of citizenship must also cause us to reflect on the impact of choice in the system, particularly the impact on those who do not have the ability to participate in the market because they lack the necessary resources, or the personal capacity, or because the system is biased. Whilst there is evidence that parents want choice, there is only limited evidence to suggest that parental choice increases pupil achievement, or brings about fundamental educational changes in schools (Woods, 1993; Goldring, Hawley, Suffold and Smrekar, 1994).

School choice reinforces social class segregation. Middle-class parents choose schools which other middle-class parents have already chosen (Goldring, 1994; Ball, Bowe and Gerwitz, 1992) and there is evidence that the education market is becoming more segmented as advantaged schools and advantaged parents seek each other out (Ranson, 1993). An investigation into the impact of school choice programmes in the US concluded that increasing parental choice accelerates both the social stratification of schools, and the gap in student performance between schools with high concentrations of poor and working-class students, as against those with predominantly white middle-class students (Fuller and Elmore, with Orfield, 1996). There is growing evidence in the UK of the link between poverty and educational failure and how past policies have contributed to this. The Catholic Education Service, for example, criticized the impact of competition and drew attention to the growing divide between affluent and deprived areas (Catholic Education Service, 1997). There is evidence too that schools which have faced financial losses under the funding formulae for schools (because of changes in student numbers) have also tended to be those which draw students from the most disadvantaged sections of the community (Bartlett, 1994).

The evidence to date is that the model of school choice promoted by the Conservative Governments has perpetuated inequalities in our education system, and created winners and losers. The winners are those parents who have the energy and 'know-how' to promote the individual rights of their child. The losers are those parents whose children have the greatest needs — which includes children with behavioural difficulties who increasingly risk exclusion from school. Some of the winners and losers are obvious, others less so. Grant-maintained (GM) schools, particularly those in the first wave, received distinct financial advantages, benefiting their school communities but disadvantaging neighbouring school communities. These financial advantages were introduced as part of an incentive by the Conservative Government to encourage grant-maintained status. The threat of and actuality of GM has also created a number of funding pressures on local authorities and even amongst local authority maintained schools there have been winners and losers[1].

But can choice and the education market-place be regulated in a way that will satisfy consumer demands and also reduce, or eradicate, inequalities? Can the new consumerism be tempered to recognize that the educational consumer is not the same as the supermarket shopper and cannot exercise the right not to buy commodities in the same way? Certainly, rectifying some of the inequalities of core funding which exist between local authority and central government funded schools, could create a more equitable framework[2]. It is difficult to justify a system which allows grant-maintained schools to apply for technology grants but not local authority maintained schools and we must ask politicians:

Can the use of public funds which aggravate divisions in our society be justified? Can we accept our role in a system which requires some children to lose out, so that others can win?[3] What does a public education service do about the losers? If choice is likely to remain an enduring feature of our system, the issue now confronting us is: '**what kinds of choice should policy promote, with what constraints and for what purposes?**' (Elmore and Fuller, 1996, p. 188).

The impact of school choice was one of the factors which confronted me when in 1997 I embarked on a project on school failure with a colleague (Riley and Rowles, 1997a). 'School failure' (defined as schools which had failed the Ofsted inspection process and had been designated as in need of 'special measures') comes about through a complex range of factors. Some are to do with the schools themselves; some to do with the impact of national policies; and some to do with socio-economic factors of poverty and deprivation. In the schools we looked at there were issues of weak leadership and poor professional practices which clearly have to be tackled. However, many of the schools were also struggling to deal with the children that other schools chose not to have. The secondary schools were frequently in competition with selective grammar, or grant-maintained schools, and as a result of local market pressures, several had undergone reorganization leaving the schools divided and disaffected[4].

In our study we also found a striking degree of teacher isolation. Staff in one school were said to be 'insular and fragmented and adrift from the usual range of professional interactions' and in another they were 'isolated from colleagues in other schools'. For this the teachers themselves must take some responsibility but we also have to question how far Conservative Government policies over recent years, which have sought to establish schools as separate institutions which must compete against each other for clients, have also contributed to this state of affairs. If schools themselves are seen as individual and separate units, it is not surprising that some teachers also behave in that way (ibid.).

We found a pattern of illness and acute staffing problems. The schools were often poorly housed and frequently had to deal with high levels of deprivation. There were significant issues of school governance, examples of conflict, lack of clarity about roles, and, unsurprisingly, given the growing demands on governors, high levels of vacancies. There was also evidence of much goodwill, but governors increasingly found themselves caught between competing forces, and struggling with issues of accountability and teacher professionalism (see Chapter 7).

In the study we also looked at the impact of the Ofsted inspection process itself on those schools which had been designated as 'failing'.

Contrary to assertions from Ofsted itself, there was no evidence that the Ofsted process itself improved schools. Effective help came to the schools in our study in the form of a concerted package of support from the LEA, including a substantial injection of cash that improved the physical surroundings. However intensive support to one such school was often at the expense of less support to other schools.

We concluded that Ofsted was a crude instrument which did not of itself move schools forward. Undoubtedly, inspection has been useful in some schools which had been resistant to change. Many schools had benefited from internal use of the Ofsted criteria and the publication of examination results had forced some schools to take a long hard look at themselves and to set targets for improvement. There was a degree of validity in the claim of Conservative Governments that many schools simply did not have the information to determine how well, or badly, children were doing, or to answer the question: How do you know if this is a good school? But inspecting a school, or publishing information about it, is not the same as improving a school. For the future, we need a more defined and less costly national audit of schools; local mechanisms for intervention; and a rechannelling of resources and energy into findings ways of identifying, challenging and supporting schools before they enter the downward spiral.

Undoubtedly, Ofsted has highlighted some major failures in the system which need to be addressed, but it has rarely identified what was not already known. If the problems were already known, why were they not tackled prior to inspection? Why did LEAs not intervene? Part of the answer to this lies with the antagonism of Conservative Government towards LEAs and in the reduction in resources which has made intervention difficult. It is also fair to say that a small number of LEAs have failed in their responsibilities. Ambivalence about the the role of the LEA has made some LEAs reluctant to intervene when they should, and some schools reluctant to accept that intervention — until Ofsted circumstances force it upon them. LEAs need to be given the powers and resources to intervene more easily before things go wrong, rather than when things have gone wrong — and they need to be called to account if they fail to do this. These issues are explored more fully in the next chapter.

The Labour Inheritance

The Labour Government faces a very different set of economic and social circumstances to those of the first Thatcher Government in 1979.

The speed and pace of education change has taken us into new and unchartered terrain and Labour will need to reflect on the impact of a range of policies which have been pursued as part of the restructuring process. Several governments, including the UK Government, have pursued de-centralization, self-management, deregulation and opting out, as part of the restructuring of the public sector, based on the assumption that the wider variations and expanded choice in public sector markets would improve services.

A UK study on the experience of self-management and the opting out in education, health care and housing, found that the consequences had been mixed (Pollitt, Birchall and Putman, 1997). The majority of managers involved in self-managed units in all three of the service areas in the study believed that their organization had achieved greater autonomy. But there was a 'striking lack of convincing before-and-after data' about whether self-management had improved performance and little evidence that services had been improved by the changes[5]. Self-management had created major gaps in public accountability and whilst greater decentralization had been achieved in all three areas, it had been accompanied by a strengthening of central government powers, particularly in relation to schools and hospitals[6]. The authors concluded that self-management had neither been 'a triumph, nor a disaster' but 'easy claims that most public service managers had been "energized" and service users "empowered"', did not stand up to close scrutiny.

Another area in which tensions and contradictions abound is the financing of education. There is clear evidence that investment in education and training yields substantial returns in terms of higher productivity, increased individual well-being and wealthier societies (Alsalam and Conley, 1995). Educational attainment and employment are strongly linked and adults without upper secondary qualifications are between five and eight times more likely to be unemployed than those with upper secondary, or higher education experience (OECD, 1996b). Young people who leave school early are at particular risk of unemployment and long-term economic exclusion (OECD, 1996a). However, Adam Smith's assertion in the *Wealth of Nations* of the importance of the relationship between education and the performance of the economy has been challenged. Economists such as Eric Hanushek now argue against the notion of investment in education as a 'general good' and suggest instead that investment needs to be closely linked to outcomes, and financial incentives linked to performance (Hanushek, 1994). Governments are questioning what are the most effective points at which they should be investing, and what reasonable returns can they expect from their investment. As parents themselves experience more formal education, so too their expectations and aspirations will continue to grow about the opportunities for their own children. The financing of education, particularly higher education, will become an even more contested issue in the twenty-first century[7,8].

Surveying the Terrain

Labour's inheritance has to be seen in the context of global challenges and the demands which a technological and knowledge-based society will make on our thinking about teaching and learning. 'Globalization' is the word that is now used to describe movements that have the power to override national frontiers and cultural identities. When we talk of world-wide change, we no longer exclude large geographical areas, or percentages of the world population. The collapse of the Berlin Wall, the end of the Cold War, the global spread of capitalism and new poverty in Western countries erode many previous distinctions between countries (Albrow, 1994). Information technology is an integral part of globalization and provides access to information which transcends national boundaries.

Globalization, along with accelerated change and greater diversity within communities, makes it increasingly difficult for national governments to predict, or influence, labour market trends. In the globalized world, multinational companies have the most power to override national frontiers and cultural identities. The free access of information on the scale offered by the Internet and interactive technology promotes the flow of both information and disinformation, knowledge that is anti-educational, as well as educational: anti-social, as well as beneficial to society (MacBeath, Moos and Riley, 1996). Education leaders will need to come to terms with the global impact of social and economic change, as well as the ways in which change is mediated by local circumstances. Schools will retain their distinctiveness, but at the same time they will also be influenced by a range of common external factors.

The challenges for teaching and learning are complex. All education institutions will face diverse and growing demands from individuals and employers which will be shaped by expectations of lifelong learning. Knowledge and information will play an even more central role in every aspect of life and will no longer be the prerogative of education institutions. Avenues to learning will need to be accessible to a wide community and a greater focus on distance and self-directed learning will be required. The learning environment will extend far beyond the confines of the classroom and students will need to be freed from the constraints of time and place (Duguet, 1995).

The prevailing culture of teaching and learning has been aptly described in an Organization for Economic Cooperation and Development (OECD) review as one in which 'necessary knowledge, competences and values are predefined and stored in curricula, tests and accredited textbooks'. It is fundamentally a static conceptualization of society which assumes a stable labour market, with relatively unchanging demands on the work force, and a requirement for 'diligent young people who have a sense of duty and discipline' Posch (1996, p. 4). The needs and challenges for the twenty-first century are very different. Roles and relationships will be more fluid and less prescribed and we will need to question what it means to prepare young people for a society in which change and acceleration, and not continuity and certainty, are the norm.

Education will face diverse and growing demands from individuals and employers which will be shaped by expectations of lifelong learning. Students increasingly have, and will bring with them, changing expectations about the role of the teacher. The 'negotiation culture' which exists in many homes will be at odds with the 'command culture' in many schools. The routes and access to knowledge will change and the boundaries between subjects, classroom activities and the world outside cease to exist. The relationship between schools and the wider community will change. Knowledge and information will play an even more central role in every aspect of life and will no longer be the prerogative of education institutions. Teachers will lose their monopoly over education.

Young people will need to be prepared for a society in which the boundaries between work and non-work will become less clear, and where individuals will move in and out of employment, training and education. The skills and capacities which they will require for the future include: the ability to cooperate and work in teams; the ability to communicate in one's mother tongue and at least one other language; the ability to identify and solve problems; media literacy; and techniques for life-long learning. Schools will need to ask themselves: 'How can (we) become more effective at fostering the development of students as autonomous, self-regulating, and self-evaluating learners and at enabling them to construct their own futures?' (ibid. p. 5).

There is a strong perception amongst many OECD countries that there is a problem of failure and under performance. Undoubtedly, school failure, drop out and poor performance will have a continuing impact on the lives of young people. Students from disadvantaged backgrounds are at a significant risk of failing in all OECD countries.

Regardless of the source of the difficulties experienced at school, there is a large difference in all OECD education systems between the level attained by the weakest 25 per cent of pupils, and the level attained by the strongest 25 per cent in the same grade (Kovacs, 1997). Generally this difference is equivalent to more than two years of schooling and in some countries amounts to as much as five years. The links between successful learning in childhood and youth, and the motivation and capacity to continue learning through later life, are very strong. Those who are excluded from the foundations for learning will also increasingly be excluded from society and, in this context, learning assumes even greater importance: it is the necessary insurance against exclusion and marginality.

Exclusion manifests itself in a number of ways, including the ways in which we organize our schools and our teaching groups and the expectations that we have of young children. It requires vigilance on the part of educators to identify both overt and subtle forms of exclusion. Technology, for example, increasingly represents an area in which the divisions are growing between the skilled and confident middle-class net-surfers, and the working-class children who do not have the access of their privileged peers to computers.

Discussions about failure and exclusion lead into a broader discussion about lifelong learning. Many countries, including the UK, have paid lip-service to lifelong learning, in order to stimulate the conditions for economic growth but fulfilling the 'active learning potential' of individuals will also increase social cohesion, by systematically widening opportunities (OECD, 1996a). The realization of the goal of lifelong learning which will require radical improvements and rethinking at all levels in an education system, raises many issues for policy-makers. In particular, there is a risk of polarization between those who are included in the new vision of education and training and those who are excluded by their limited education experience, or by restricted training opportunities. Many training programmes *permit* access to particular kinds of opportunities but are no more than 'parking mechanisms' which offer limited prospects for active learning, or to gain the skills and knowledge needed to improve both life and career chances (OECD, 1995a).

In thinking about lifelong learning, we also need to look at the transition from school to work — no longer a short crossing but a continuous journey. Work carried out by the OECD suggests that policy-makers will need to look not only at the transition from school to work but at patterns of drop-out and exclusion, and at the kinds of vocational preparation which will succeed for young people themselves, and for society in general. Some of the issues which need to be taken account of are as follows.

- The main period of transition from school to work averages about six years in OECD countries. It has not increased in the past decade, but it has been delayed — starting in the late teens and ending by the mid-twenties.
- During this transition, many young people are simultaneously students and workers — up to half of 16 to 19 year-olds in some countries (including the UK) although far fewer in others. The biggest growth has been in full-time students working part-time rather than in the more traditional form of combining work and study through an apprenticeship.
- Young people who drop out without finishing upper second-ary education face severe long-term risks on the job market. Although youth unemployment has fallen in some countries, a growing number of teenagers, particularly young women, drop out of both the labour market and education.
- In some countries, young people continue to build skills and competences after they enter work; in others they appear to lose them.
- Vocational preparation that is well supported by employers is less likely to be followed by unemployment than either general education, or school-oriented vocational education. But every-where there is a need to reduce divisions between general and vocational education, and to improve pathways between dif-ferent kinds of programmes. (McKenzie, 1997)

A New Agenda for Labour?

The reforms of the 1980s and early 1990s which were part of the Thatcher legacy were concerned to a large degree with structure: how schools were to be financed and governed; curriculum specified; pupil perform-ance assessed. Changes will be needed in some of the structural arrange-ments if issues of equity are to be tackled. We will also need to find answers to some difficult questions. If education is to be able to provide young people with the opportunities to gain the skills and knowledge that they need *and* take responsibility for their own learning, what steps will need to be taken? If teachers are to be enthused and inspired and acquire a greater sense of their own professional contribution to the educational process, how will this happen? If new forms of partnership are to be forged between central and local government, and between local government, schools and the communities which they serve, what changes in attitudes and expectations will be required?

Undoubtedly, Margaret Thatcher and 'Thatcherism' have changed our thinking about education in many ways. Egalitarian philosophies and aspirations have been squeezed out in favour of individual enterprise and consumer rights. Providing some mediation in that choice which safeguards the losers and the have-nots in our society will have the effect of reducing the choices for some — a politician's nightmare. For when we ask the question 'whose school is it anyway?' we are forced to make some important value judgments.

In July 1997, David Blunkett, Secretary of State for Education and Employment presented to the House of Commons the Labour Government's White Paper, *Excellence in Schools* — the basis for consultation in the autumn of 1997, and legislation in 1998. He described the Paper as 'a new partnership for schools — one with teachers and the profession'.

> Self-improvement is at the core of success. Schools must take responsibility for accepting that challenge. Good schools will flourish. Our proposals offer increased support through the new Standards and Effectiveness Unit to schools in need of improvement. (Hansard, 1997a)

Stephen Byers, Minister for School Standards, explained to the House that there were six principles behind the White Paper proposals.

> First, education will be at the heart of the Government . . . Secondly, we want policies designed to benefit the many, not just the few. The third principle that underpins the White Paper is that we have made it clear that standards matter more than structures. The fourth . . . is that intervention will be in inverse proportion to success . . . Linked to this is the fifth principle: there will be zero tolerance of under performance . . . The sixth principle is that the Government will work in partnership with all those committed to higher standards. (Hansard, 1997b)

The White Paper contained proposals for a nursery place for all 4 year olds and maximum class sizes of 30 for 5–7 year olds. The drive for standards included a compulsory hour/day for both maths and English in primary schools; proposals for national standards for teachers (including an advanced skills teacher grade); and a General Teaching Council to 'regulate and promote' the profession (see Chapter 9). The new headteachers' qualification was to become a mandatory requirement. Schools would be required to set 'challenging' targets for improvement and LEAs to produce development plans to show how standards in schools would rise. The notice which schools were given in advance of an Ofsted inspection period would be shortened and schools which were designated as 'failing' the inspection could close, or possible reopen with different staff. There would be an end to Easter leavers (i.e. young people who left school before the end of their final year). There would be annual rewards for the most improved school — described by one newspaper as a 'Cash-for results-scheme' (Evening Standard, 1997) and 'Action Zones' to tackle under performance in disadvantaged areas. The Paper emphasized traditional teaching methods and while there was to be no selection by ability for entry to secondary school, 'setting' rather than mixed ability teaching would become the standard practice:

> Unless a school can demonstrate that it is getting better than expected results through a different approach, we do make the assumption that setting should be the norm. (White Paper, 1997, p. 38)

The Paper contained a chapter on parental roles in education and suggested that a central feature of the home-school relationship would be home-school contracts — about discipline, attendance and the kinds of information which parents could expect from the school[9]. There were also proposals for more parent-governors, for parent representatives on the LEA, and for fuller information to parents about school performance. The Paper contained proposals about the status of schools which were aimed at resolving differences between the funding and governance arrangements of grant-maintained and other schools. Schools would be 'able to choose the status which would best suit their character and aspirations' (ibid. p. 7, see note 10).

The newspaper headlines which greeted the publication of the White Paper highlighted the drive towards improving standards and the likely impact of this on teachers:

Schools Blitz as Blunkett Goes Back to Basics (Daily Express, 1997)

Labour Targets Teachers in Drive to Improve Standards (Daily Telegraph, 1997a)

The Guardian, often described as the teachers' paper, led its coverage with, 'Ambitious' Plan Excites Teachers' but despite this headline, went on to describe the Government as having 'won the first round of the battle to raise standards in schools'. The White Paper threatened 'draconian penalties for under performance' (Guardian, 1997b). Union leaders were reported as having given a cautious welcome to aspects of the Paper — particularly directed towards the promise of increased resources and the commitment to reduce class sizes. However, Nigel de Gruchy from the National Association of Schoolmasters, Union of Women Teachers warned of overload, 'my chief fear is whether . . . the teaching profession will be able to survive another huge dose of medicine' (ibid.).

The move away from progressive teaching methods was described by the *Evening Standard* as:

> Labour turns its back on years of 'trendy' teaching . . . Labour was today discarding three decades of trendy education theories in favour of traditional methods and tough new targets in Britain's schools. (Evening Standard, 1997)

The *Financial Times* reported this shift as Labour having learned 'Lessons from the old school' (1997a); but the *Daily Mail* dismissed the White Paper as rhetoric, 'Blunkett's great classroom gamble . . . Fine words, but the old rotten dogmas will stay', (Daily Mail, 1997a); and, in a front page splash, condemned Labour's plan to ban selection for secondary school places (Daily Mail, 1997b).

One of the quandaries posed by the White Paper is how much control the state should assume and how much should be left to other parties — an issue which is discussed in the concluding chapter. The *Independent*'s headline (reported in Chapter 1) captured elements of this dilemma, 'Government to have its hand in every school' (1997a), which was also echoed in other columns of the *Independent*, and in other papers. Judith Judd, Education Editor of the *Independent* warned of the dangers of the centralization of powers and speculated about the consequences if some of the proposals in the White Paper became law. 'How many officials will be needed to scrutinize targets and development plans for school improvement, early years education and class-size reduction? . . . Will the entire Department for Education drown in a morass of paperwork?' (Independent, 1997b). The *Daily Telegraph* in an editorial argued that whilst the Tories had left the raising of standards to 'the invisible hand of competition', Education Secretary David Blunkett 'intends to thrust his own hand directly into the classroom, with a series of government initiatives ranging from teacher training to homework' (Daily Telegraph, 1997b). The *Economist* concluded that 'Mr Blunkett will be more prescriptive than any of his predecessors' (Economist, 1997).

Reflecting on the White Paper, Peter Wilby identified three major gaps which in his view would need to be 'plugged' if permanent improvement was to take place: an improvement in teacher morale, tackling the multiple problems of underachievement in inner cities, and closing the gap between the worst and the best performing schools (Wilby, 1997a). The White Paper undoubtedly offers some new perceptions of education which reflect the changing political agenda. It shows a spirited determination by Government to keep education high on the political agenda, but whether it offers a sufficient basis for success in the twenty-first century will depend on a range of factors — including, above all, the willingness of the Government to allow others to play their part.

Notes

1   Over recent years in many parts of the country, there had been the beginnings of a shift in the balance of funding between secondary and primary schools, with primary schools making some gains. This shift has come to a halt, or has been reversed in a number of local authorities because the threat of GM (largely perceived as a threat from secondary schools) has driven LEAs towards funding secondary schools, as closely as possible, to the level estimated by central government in the block allocation to local authorities: the standard spending assessment (SSA). The SSA formula tends to favour secondary schools, at the expense of primary. This trend came to light in an ESRC project, funded under its Local Governance Programme, and carried out by Stephen Smith and colleagues at University College, London.

2   Even advocates of school autonomy and school choice such as Chubb and Moe (1990) concede that choice needs to be regulated.

3   Geoff Whitty in an an overview of the literature on 'parental choice' and 'school autonomy' in Britain, New Zealand and America argues that more attention needs to be given to 'mechanisms of regulation and to the most appropriate ways of deciding them' (Whitty, 1997, p. 36).

4   These findings have been backed up by a study by the Child Poverty Action Group which has put forward evidence to suggest that market forces have worked against poorer children and that, in particular areas of the country, there are schools with growing numbers of disadvantaged children, some of whom have been excluded by other schools (CPAG, 1997; Dawson and Riley, 1997).

5   There does not appear to be empirical or research evidence from elsewhere to suggest that school-based management has increased student achievement. A major study on the impact of local management of schools in England and Wales conducted over a three year period found that the majority of headteachers were broadly positive about the impact of LMS but that evidence of the impact of LMS on outcomes was 'elusive' (Arnott, Bullock and Thomas, 1992).

6   One of the consequences of decentralization in education has been that local authorities with significant numbers of grant-maintained schools are

no longer in a position to plan sensibly for the needs of their area (Pollitt, Birchall and Putman, 1997).

7   The finance of higher education became a source of intense media interest in the summer of 1997 when some of the consequences of Government plans to introduce annual tuition fees of £1,000 a year from October 1998 were revealed. Controversy centred on those students who had planned to take a 'gap-year' before taking a degree (i.e. they had won a place but had deferred it for a year). The Government finally agreed to waive charges for this group in what was reported as a 'retreat after gap-year fiasco' (Times Higher Education Supplement, 1997).

8   The UK Government will also need to tackle complex issues about the financing of local government and the extent to which it wishes to pursue a policy of equalization of resources. A policy of equalization would require central government to fund local government on the basis of the needs of different localities and their tax base. However, since the introduction of the Community Charge in the late 1980s, central government has moved away from full equalization to what has been described as 'point equalization' which puts local authorities on a common footing to spend at the same level (Smith, 1997). A policy of full equalization would allocate education resources to local authorities on the basis of need — benefiting inner city urban areas such as Tower Hamlets — but such a policy would be at odds with a commitment to reduce class sizes for all young children across the country, regardless of social need.

9   The White Paper proposals for home-school contracts (which were to be compulsory — although not legally binding) were dismissed in 1997 by the Campaign for State Education as a 'quick-fix solution, part of the blame culture which seems to pervade current educational thinking' (TES, 1997b). The relationship between parents and schools is discussed in Chapter 9, including home-school contracts.

10 The proposed creation of three types of state schools has proved to be controversial. Roy Hattersley has argued that the different categories will create a 'hierarchy of schools' with parents seeing foundation status, the new status for grant-maintained schools, as superior to that of community status, the likely status of most LEA schools (Hattersley, 1997).

Part II

Reconstructing the Reform Agenda for the Twenty-first Century

Chapter 7

Whose School — The Local Authority's or the Governors'?

Schools are increasingly atomizing rather than working together. Headteachers treat each other with suspicion because of the competition between schools. There are less formal networks and no informal networks which attempt to disseminate good practice. There is little informal professional collaboration. At one time there would have been a sense that we are in a tough job together . . . that's gone. League tables reflect the nature of the problem. It has become a zero sum game. If your school is doing better then you don't need to collaborate. If its doing worse, then other schools don't want to collaborate with you . . . Schools don't collaborate because there is no prospect of new markets. Local government officer (quoted in Riley, 1997, p. 162)

In the next three chapters I want to move away from the broader national concerns and questions to focus on schools in their local contexts and to look at roles and relationships between LEAs, schools and governors, and between schools, parents and children. I want to consider what say each should have in what goes on in our schools.

Checks and Balances

Schools enjoyed a large degree of independence for the first three decades of the post-war era. They were seen by consecutive Conservative and Labour governments as benign institutions, pursuing the public good. Education was to be delivered through a professionally-driven model which was heavily dependent on trust. Central government trusted local education authorities to deliver policy objectives. LEAs in their turn entrusted teachers with the task of devising and delivering the education experience.

Events at Tyndale exposed serious flaws in this relationship of mutual dependency and trust. As Peter Newsam has argued in Chapter 3, the local authority found itself caught in a trap. On the one hand was its determination to break free of the authoritarian traditions of the past in which affairs were largely directed by County Hall, in favour of a policy of open devolvement of control to governors. On the other hand, its commitment to encouraging teacher autonomy and professional control was based on a belief that this would maximize creativity in the classroom. The ILEA was caught between the need to democratize and the need to retain accountability.

The ILEA's unwillingness to spell out the power relations between parents, governors and the local authority sprang from a belief that there were common interests and shared understandings in education. Tyndale challenged that assumption and demonstrated that views were contested. The governors were in conflict with the teachers. The wishes of many of the parents at Tyndale were at variance with those of the teachers. The education of children was in jeopardy but the local authority did not see its role as intervening in the school on behalf of parents and children. The LEA view was that the remedy lay within the school itself, teachers and governors.

The assumption that there was broad agreement amongst differing parties about educational objectives, and that attitudes were shared, was a prevailing national belief for many years in the post-war period. It was reflected in the power settlement between central and local governments and the assumptions which lay behind it. R.A. Butler, responsible under Winston Churchill for drawing up the 1944 Education Act, described the settlement as one in which the Minister remained responsible to Parliament for 'policy' and relied on local education authorities for the administration of that policy. The scope and variety of the provision depended on 'local initiative' (Hansard, 1944). Writing in the 1950s, Sir William Pile, Permanent Secretary at the Ministry of Education, concurred with this view and described the relationship in the following terms:

> We (in Whitehall) did not plan education itself. Curricular, pedagogical and professional matters are by a long tradition in this country matters in which the State does not take control . . . Town Halls and County Halls plan and provide teachers to nurture the process of learning in accordance with parents' wishes. (Quoted in Buxton, 1973, p. 101)

The relationship between central government, local government and schools — the triangle of checks and balances — continued for two decades, rudely challenged by the grammar/comprehensive school controversy of the 1960s and 1970s (see Chapter 2). According to pundits of the day, under the conflicting pressures, relationships became a 'confused co-existence between national and local government' which enabled Whitehall to 'procrastinate and confuse the public as to who was responsible for policy-making, even if in the process the policy-makers became confused themselves' (ibid. p. 105). Whether there was clarity or obfuscation, local government throughout that period was a major player in the education game.

Local government in Britain is, however, a creature of statute — an invention of central government — and what government makes, it can also unmake. And unmake, to a large degree, it did. The legitimacy of local government as a major player in education was challenged by the 1988 Education Reform Act and further eroded by the attitudes of successive Secretaries of State for Education and by subsequent legislation. At the heart of the challenge was a belief by national politicians that local politicians and education professionals were responsible for the failure of the education system. For reform solutions to be successful, they had to be consumer-focused and centrally directed.

Throughout the later 1980s and into the 1990s, LEAs were caught in a pincer movement. National Government increasingly assumed new powers and sought to devolve existing LEA responsibilities to schools and governing bodies, and to shift the locus of decision-making away from the producer to the consumer. Through national inspection and tests, the Government emphasized the autonomy of schools and their accountability for performance. Schools were to be offered financial incentives to break free from local authorities and to maximize their autonomy through grant-maintained status. LEAs were not to be abolished but it was assumed that as their responsibilities, resources and prestige diminished, they would wither on the vine.

In 1991, Kenneth Clarke, Secretary of State for Education, announced to a Conservative Local Government Conference, 'I do not believe that day to day management of schools should be carried out by local education authorities' (Clarke, 1991). Michael Heseltine, Secretary of State for the Environment, argued at the same conference that it would be necessary to transfer education from local authority to central government control if standards were to be improved. But the questioning of the need for a local education authority was not simply a matter of Conservative dogma. In June 1991, the *Independent* newspaper published a 'Schools' Charter' which included the following proposal:

> We recommend the eventual abolition of local education authorities — not because they are solely to blame for the performance crisis but because their role is withering away and the ground must be cleared. (Independent, 1991)

If LEAs were set to wither away, how have they fared over recent years?

LEAs Struggling for a Role

The role of LEAs has altered beyond recognition as a result of major changes in the character of public service management, and as a consequence of restructuring which has seen a movement away from a system of local government to one of local governance. Major decisions are no longer taken by the local authority largely on its own, but power and decision-making has become much more dispersed, and responsibilities are now shared with a number of public, private and voluntary sector agencies and institutions.

Post-16 provision is an area in which the complexities and tensions of local governance have become particularly acute. Training and Enterprise Councils, VI Form and Further Education Colleges, schools, local authorities, Regional Government Offices, and the Further Education Funding Council are caught up in a web of resource transactions, and compete with each other for students. The competitive and market-orientated climate drives individual institutions towards autonomy to retain their position in the market. None has the legitimacy to take a lead in the locality, and although closer cooperation on the ground could benefit students, in practice this has been difficult to achieve (Riley, 1997).

The education market has created further tensions and challenges. LEAs and schools have been forced into an exchange relationship which has contradictory elements. In a climate of dwindling powers and more devolution of resources to schools, LEAs have had to sell many of their services such as personnel advice, or advisory support to schools. This market relation has undoubtedly made it difficult for LEAs to challenge the performance of schools. Schools which are reluctant to accept the professional challenge of the LEA have been able to reject it, to opt out of LEA 'control', or to refuse to buy services.

In the context of these uncertainties, in 1993 I undertook the first of two studies on the role of the LEA and its relationship with schools (Riley, 1994b, see Note 1). Given the new power and resource configuration, what could be expected from the LEA? There were ten LEAs in the study and both LEAs and schools were struggling: LEAs sought to find a role for themselves in the new competitive environment and to establish the basis of a new relationship with schools; schools sought to meet a myriad of expectations and demands. Some LEAs still saw themselves as major players in what happened in schools. Others had concluded that the devolution of budgets to schools and the creation of Ofsted to check national standards left them with a minimal role[2].

The different roles and attitudes of the LEAs fell under four broad headings which could be seen as located on a continuum from interventionist to non-interventionist:

Interventionist<..>Interactive< ..>Responsive< ..> Non-interventionist

Prior to the introduction of Local Management of Schools (LMS), the 'interventionist' LEA, whether of the political right or political left, had been characterized by a strong quality control thrust (checks to ensure that pupils had achieved expected quality standards). Within the context of the changes, quality control had given way to quality assurance (ways of assuring that the processes were in place which would ensure a good learning experience for children). The interventionist LEA continued to see itself as the defender of children's rights in the locality. If schools 'went off the rails' (which was something which could happen within a six month period) it would intervene at an early stage.

School self-development was encouraged but within a framework of a continued LEA inspection programme and systematic monitoring and evaluation. The interventionist LEA analysed and published local and national test information; set local and school targets for achievement; worked with schools to monitor whole school development plans; looked at their relationship to local authority-wide budgetary policies and budgetary processes. A primary head who had taken over the headship of a neighbouring school which was in difficulties described the strong leadership role of the LEA in the following terms.

> I took over a school that was failing. The head wouldn't admit that there were problems, he said that weak teachers were wonderful. The situation escalated and it was the strong intervention of the LEA which changed things. Since taking over, they've given me every kind of support.

The 'interactive' LEA was determined to improve schools by enhancing and developing the capabilities of staff. It saw schools as self-developing but not always able to evaluate what they had done on their own, or to know that they had achieved their objectives. Its own *raison d'être* was to provide educational leadership. A focus of the LEA's activities was in helping schools to develop methods of measuring improvement. The success of the LEA's strategy was dependent on fostering good relationships and providing a critical but supportive forum in which schools could evaluate their progress. The interactive LEA encouraged schools to be part of the LEA 'club', membership of which offered strong guarantees of quality assurance in schools.

Inspection remained part of the LEA's role but as part of a wider strategy to evaluate effectiveness. The LEA aimed to bring together the outcomes from inspection with realistic and situational specific information and to feed this back to schools. School evaluation was carried out jointly by the LEA and schools and drew on criteria which had been developed in partnership. The interactive relationship between the LEA and its schools was critical and it was through this that a shared vision could be created. The services provided by the interactive LEA were valued by its headteachers.

> We haven't the time to shop about but we have a broad measure of trust in our local services . . . They provide local legitimacy and a local voice . . . but it's not just the product, it's the process.

The 'responsive' LEA had taken a more distant and uncertain role in quality through a combination of diminishing resources and the presence of a number of opted-out schools. However, it was experiencing change and headteachers were beginning to exert their influence, and to demand a more proactive role on the part of the LEA. A group of primary heads in one local authority with a high number of opted-out schools wrote a letter to the local newspaper to explain why they wanted to remain linked to the LEA:

> Local accountability is an essential part of community education . . . There is a strong sense of belonging which is an essential element in providing a high quality service . . . The professionals we rely on have a strong sense of commitment to us which would go if the service was sold out. Heads, staff and governors should have access to locally coordinated induction, development and on-going support which has a local focus.

The 'responsive' LEA was struggling to provide a vision and to offer direction to schools — if that was what schools wanted — and was having to deal with the criticism from schools that it had been reactive rather than proactive in the past. In managing these tensions, it was seeking to challenge the isolation of schools and offer a perspective on quality that reflected local purposes. Research, analysis, customer surveys and information that would enable schools to bench-mark their progress were frequently part of this strategy. Schools needed to be curriculum leaders, 'wise customers,' in the new entrepreneurial environment but protected from the worst excesses of the market.

The 'non-interventionist' LEA had put the bulk of its services out into the market place some time ago. It had withdrawn its own inspection services, as elected members thought objectivity could only be provided by inspection which was external to the authority. It argued that the quality framework set by central government and the inspection arrangements through Ofsted, would largely ensure that standards were maintained. Schools were seen as autonomous, responsible for their own successes and failures. As the LEA had made the decision to maximize the devolution of resources to schools, quality became the direct responsibility of schools.

The role of the LEA was limited to developing key indicators which could throw contextual light on specific areas of performance, or expenditure. National information on standard assessment tasks, public examinations and truancy were to be used as the major indicators of school performance. This information would also be made available, as widely as possible, to parents. The LEA no longer retained a capacity to support development work in schools, or to support an action programme following an Ofsted inspection. This was seen as the responsibility of the autonomous schools themselves. Critics identified some inherent weaknesses in this model.

> The problem about the new system is that schools can easily go adrift without the support of a semi-detached visitor . . . Schools know very little about guaranteeing quality, it's partly our fault that we haven't trained them to do this.

In a follow up study in 1995, we found that a number of changes had taken place (Riley, Johnson and Rowles, 1995; Riley and Rowles, 1997b). Competition had undoubtedly sharpened the consciousness of LEAs of the need to provide good quality services and the expectations of schools that high quality services should be delivered. A new climate was evolving — partly in response to the nationally set agenda — in which evaluation and monitoring had become the norm, but also in response to a strong assertion of common educational goals at the local level and a wish to develop collaboration rather than competition. A settling down period had taken place between schools and LEAs and the substance, rather than the rhetoric of the partnership, was beginning to evolve. What went on in schools was beginning to be seen as the business of schools (governors and headteacher) and of the LEA. LEAs were becoming more, not less, involved in what was happening in schools and there was movement along the continuum in the direction shown:

**Interventionist<<<Interactive<<<Responsive<<<
Non-interventionist <<<**

Movement along the continuum did not represent an increase in levels of services but rather a change in attitude or approach and a targeting of limited resources towards specific activities. However, there were also many uncertainties. There were issues to do with officer/member relationships; there were issues to do with school governance; there were issues to do with the leadership of the LEA; and there were issues to do with the nature of intervention. When should the LEA intervene? What legitimacy did it have to do so and on whose behalf should it intervene?

LEAs: Finding a Voice

In the project on school failure described in the previous chapter, we looked at the characteristics of 'failing schools' and the lessons to be learned (Riley and Rowles, 1997a). We found that a number of the schools in serious difficulties had been reluctant to accept the advice and criticism of the LEA prior to Ofsted inspection. The authority's right to support, improve, or, if necessary, remove headteachers, teachers, or even governors had become a grey area and the notion of intervention was associated with a past era in which LEAs had been seen as too controlling.

Where LEAs had stepped into the grey area and challenged boundaries, they had frequently been hampered by their reduced capacity to effect improvement. LEAs had been caught out in the Ofsted conundrum: seeking national inspection contracts to bring in resources and increase credibility, but by so doing, reducing the amount of time that they could spend within their own schools. Smaller LEAs, in particular, were struggling to carry out the range of tasks required of them. A few LEAs had simply not grasped what their role was and had failed to have an impact locally.

The tensions and difficulties at school level were mirrored by contradictory pressures at national level. Kenneth Clarke and Michael Heseltine might have wanted to see an end of the LEA but Gillian

Shephard, the Secretary of State for Education until 1997, was more ambivalent. She had strong connections with local government (having served as a local adviser to schools and as a local politician) and recognized that the successful implementation of national objectives (such as the introduction of changes to the National Curriculum, as recommended by Sir Ron Dearing) depended to some degree on the LEA. In 1996, she introduced an Education White Paper which became the basis of legislation in 1997. The White Paper set out National Government's expectations about schools, and to some extent their expectations about LEAs. It supported a strong line of individual school autonomy but also reaffirmed a role for the LEA.

> The Government intends schools to have as much independence as possible. The role of local education authorities will be to provide services which schools cannot carry out for themselves and to support schools in their effort to raise standards. (White Paper, 1996, p. 11)

> The Government's priority is to foster the internal will and capacity of schools to generate their own improvement . . . staff and governors of every school should feel that it is directly for them to monitor the quality of the education they provide and improve schools . . . There should be a presumption against any external intervention which detracts from this. (ibid. p. 53)

However, the White Paper also placed a strong emphasis on advice and support services and the provision of performance data which would help schools set their own targets for improvement. LEAs were to provide this assistance through direct intervention where a school is found to have a major problem; through working with schools in setting targets; and through the provision of services to help schools carry out their own plans for improvement.

The 1996 White Paper also acknowledged the need for a broader role for LEAs and suggested that the local authority was well-placed to coordinate networks of headteachers and governors; develop new initiatives which would bring schools together; and link schools with other local agencies, such as TECs. The need to develop networks which would create integration and coherence in an increasingly fragmented system, is of growing importance. The Paper signalled — if somewhat belatedly — a recognition that schools cannot function as isolated units. Yet the education system over recent years has been characterized by fragmentation and isolation.

The election of a Labour Government in 1997 put the spotlight back on LEAs. They have not withered on the vine as many predicted.

The change of government and the beginnings of new thinking on teaching and learning suggest that a dynamic review of the role of LEAs is likely to emerge. This new role will be vitally important in establishing a positive and creative partnership with schools (teachers and governors) and other parts of the education service. The Labour White Paper (1997) identified a leadership role for the LEA which is dependent upon the ability of the LEA to win 'the trust and respect of schools' and champion 'the value of education in its community for adults as well as children' (White Paper, 1997, p. 69). Each LEA will be required to draw up development plans which should indicate how the LEA works with schools and how it will help schools to establish 'robust mechanisms for self-evaluation' (DfEE, 1997)[3].

As part of their new legitimacy, LEAs are to be subject to inspection. But this inspection business is not new. In the days of Keith Joseph, HMI turned its attention to LEAs and carried out a number of studies, the most controversial of which was the study on Brent which focused on the overall impact of the authority's race policies, following press allegations of 'race spies in the classroom' (DES, 1987). The studies attempted to build up a template of questions which examined issues of quality and effectiveness and aimed to illuminate practices and outcomes, although HMI had no power to investigate administrative arrangements, or executive and policy-making practices. The LEA inspections were gradually abandoned, however, as Government thinking moved away from the LEA system to the sub-system (i.e. schools).

LEAs need to be called to account and an external evaluation of their performance is an important element of that. But we need to guard against an inspection process which is excessively costly, overly prescriptive and which is aimed primarily at exposing weaknesses, rather than tackling problems. As with school inspection, it is easier to inspect than to improve. The issue of LEA effectiveness is a complicated one and made more so by the devolution of responsibilities to schools and governing bodies. We need to start by looking at the potential benefits to schools of being part of the LEA.

There are at least four general models of the school/LEA relationship which express the nature of those benefits. The first is a 'service' model based on an economic formulation of the relationship: the schools receive valuable services from the LEA of higher quality than they could afford if they had opted out. Such services might include, for example, financial or other types of management, building maintenance, or computing.

The second is sociological and is suggested by the use of the term 'membership': affiliation with the LEA provides some 'benefits' to the school of the kind that members typically got from organizations to which they belonged. The term 'benefits', like 'services', has economic overtones but it is used to try to capture anything within the school/ LEA relationship which is positively perceived, such as the opportunity to discuss common problems with colleagues from different schools or LEAs, and to hear about the successful practices from elsewhere. The third model is political: association with the LEA provides the school with access to power or influence in its dealings with the outside world — the DfEE, the NUT, the wider local authority, the community. Schools could lose this association in the relatively isolated world of grant-maintained status.

The fourth model is educational leadership: association with the LEA provides support for curricular improvement in teaching and learning, perhaps within the 'pressure and support' paradigm familiar from studies of educational change in schools and school districts in North America. The inspection and advisory work of the LEA would probably be the main source of assistance with the appraisal of teachers, support for change, review of the curriculum and school objectives as other important elements (Coleman and Riley, 1995). The four models are not mutually exclusive and, indeed, schools may be able to maximize the benefits of LEA membership by being able to draw on all four.

It is also possible to look at the LEA in terms of its effectiveness. With colleagues, I have been trying to explore this in a study which has concentrated primarily upon the relationship between LEAs and schools, but has also looked at the LEA's broader role of providing and supporting services to the wider community[4]. Our particular concern has been to identify ways in which the relationship enhances, or detracts from, the effectiveness of schools. We have looked at the issue of effectiveness from the perspective of users and providers of services and focused on three particular components. Is the LEA:

- efficiently managed?
- responsive to needs?
- improvement orientated?

The evidence so far is that if services are 'efficiently managed', then schools feel that they are being treated equitably, and parents and students feel that the LEA has planned well for their needs. Those LEAs which are seen to be 'responsive to needs' give equal opportunities and access to learning a high priority. Governors feel that the LEA takes account of their interests and provides them with high quality services which enable them to carry out their role more effectively. An LEA which is responsive is also able to listen to and understand both the local and national contexts.

The effective LEA has to be efficiently managed and responsive to needs but it also has to be 'improvement orientated'. An LEA which is improvement orientated is highly supportive. It initiates new developments and focuses on improving achievement. It has well developed systems for monitoring school improvement and quality which help individual learners to maximize their potential. An LEA that is improvement orientated sets the framework for teaching and learning in its locality. It is clear about its plans for the future and it knows when and how to intervene. It would not hesitate to intervene in a Tyndale-type situation. Bringing the two constructs together as a scale of benefits and a scale of effectiveness, it will be possible to gain a broad measure of the role of the LEA and its achievements.

There are, however, other aspects of the relationship than those mapped on the two scales. There are issues to do with advocacy, protection and arbitration. The LEA takes responsibility for safeguarding the rights of individual students and parents. Where necessary, it mediates in local disputes between governors and teachers, teachers and parents. By endeavouring to take an overarching responsibility for admissions procedures, exclusions and the provision of special needs, it attempts to balance the rights of individuals against the needs and demands of schools and the broader community.

There are also issues concerned with the broad leadership of the service which are to do with promotion of a wider vision of education. Such leadership is about taking risks, sharing in learning, thinking the unthinkable, being willing to intervene and being clear about the reasons for intervention and the methods. It is about the ability to make connections between the demands of the labour market, changing global contexts, and the community context for learning which finds expression in the internal world of the school. It is also about building a broad education partnership with parents and pupils, governors and schools, other education institutions and the local business and wider community. Educational leadership of this sort has many elements. Some, such as clear strategy and communications, are common to good management elsewhere. However, there are also some features which are intrinsic to public service which are about mediating; defining and making value judgments about the common good[5]; and offering a clearly articulated professional lead based on these values.

The LEA needs to set high expectations about success, and challenge failure and exclusion. Life-long learning and new pathways and opportunities to learning for as many as possible through open-learning and access to technology need to be high priorities. The local environment should be one which supports teaching and learning, and in which teachers are valued for their contribution but are also challenged in their thinking. The LEA needs to be clear about what it is trying to achieve, how it goes about achieving it, and whether it has any means of measuring whether it has achieved its goals.

How LEAs manifest their leadership role in relation to schools, and how it is perceived by schools, is critical. In an analysis of American urban schools, Karen Seashore Louis and Sharon Kruse (1995) have argued that the politics of control at district level have consumed the energy of American school leaders, distracting them from their primary task of developing a professional community. School leaders in a Canadian study tended to see the policies and procedures of the local district as hurdles to be overcome (Leithwood, Begley and Cousins, 1994, p. 249). Similarly, Peter Coleman and Linda LaRocque (1990), in an earlier Canadian study on school districts, concluded that the effective districts provided support which enabled teachers and headteachers to concentrate on specific areas of student learning and on school goals. School districts, or LEAs, can be a help, but they can also be a hindrance.

Governors in the Frame[6]

While LEAs have been searching for a role, how have governors fared? The accretion of powers to governors in England and Wales over recent years has been considerable. With the introduction of local management of schools the governing bodies of LEA schools were given responsibility for the school budget; the appointment of staff; school action plans following an Ofsted inspection; and the implementation of the National Curriculum and a range of policy initiatives. Governors of grant-maintained schools were given even greater responsibilities and autonomy. In relation to staffing alone (including appointments and dismissals), seven different Acts of Parliament (and a further seven sets of Regulations) currently determine the legal parameters of what governors may do and how they may do it (Tomlinson, 1993). The Thatcher revolution served to move governing bodies into the front line of education reform — and ultimately, political debate[7].

But the school governing body is not a new invention. The 1870 Forster Education Act established school boards (embryonic local authorities) which were permitted to delegate some of their powers to the managers of elementary schools. Those early school managers had much to contend with, including disputes between parents and teachers. In

1888, a Southwark father complained to the school management committee of his daughter's school because a teacher had criticized his daughter's hair. The managers retorted that the child was an 'object of mirthful comment' on Friday afternoons as she came to school with her hair in curling papers, and concluded that 'the teacher acts correctly in endeavouring to ensure that each child should attend seemly in condition and appearance' (School Board of London Minutes, 1888, quoted in Davin, 1996, p. 137).

Elementary school managers also battled for resources, again something which the school governor of today would recognize. In turn of the century Battersea, Charlotte Despard, social reformer and suffragette and elected manager of two elementary schools, challenged the local Inspector of Education for failing, in her view, to take into account the physical condition of children in the schools (rickets, malnourishment and bare feet). Charlotte Despard's motto was 'Nourish the body and the brain will benefit' and with this in mind she set up a boot fund which in its first year bought two hundred pairs of boots for the children (Linklater, 1980, pp. 98–9).

Throughout the postwar era, the role of the school governor or manager was to provide 'oversight' of what was happening in schools. But oversight is a word which, as we saw in the case of William Tyndale, is open to very different interpretations. Events at Tyndale brought into sharp relief questions about the balance of power between local authorities, schools and school governors and created demands for a clearer settlement. The Taylor Committee was set up to bring about some resolution of these issues (Sallis, 1988). But five years after Taylor, Maurice Kogan concluded that this partnership had not been achieved and that governors were still uncertain of their role.

> Many are diffident about their ability to substitute their lay knowledge for that of professionals. While some governors think that they should ensure that the teachers account to a wider public than their own staff room, the terms of reference are shaped by the local political, community and school culture and the conventions established by key figures in and around the school. (Kogan, 1986, p. 68)

How far does this ambivalence and uncertainty prevail today on the part of governors? Evidence suggests that governors are still struggling to establish their role. Recent delegation of local authority powers and responsibilities to school governors has strengthened the influence of headteachers rather than governors. Whether headteachers will continue to dominate governing bodies in the way that they have in the past, remains to be seen (Deem, 1990). But it is also clear that head-teacher authority has also been tempered by governing bodies and there is still much to be negotiated in the relationship between the two (Mahony, 1995).

The evidence also suggests that the majority of governors carry out their role with enthusiasm, attend sub-committees, contribute to working parties, and are attached to particular curriculum areas within the school. In practice, however, few feel that they have the knowledge or confidence to question recommendations from the senior team in a school. As one chair of governors commented to me, 'We fear to tread and don't ask searching questions since this could be taken as criticism of the professionals' (Riley, Johnson and Rowles, 1995, p. 12)[8]. The problems and tensions in the role have been described in the following terms:

> *A governor's view*:   We are a group of amateurs often faced with very tricky situations.
> *An LEA officer's view*:   Most governors have neither the skills, the time, nor the willingness to carry out their intended role. Their interpretation of what makes a good school is superficial and not based on real knowledge.
> *A headteacher's view*:   The role of the governor isn't clear cut. The governors, particularly the parent governors, tend to see quality in terms of individual teacher quality.
> *A councillor's view*:   Governors are placed in an unfair situation in that they simply do not know enough to challenge management activities in schools. (ibid. p. 11)

Given the relative newness of governing bodies in their current form, it is perhaps unsurprising that such difficulties exist. Where governors are supportive the head's leadership role is enhanced. However, the accountability relationship is complex and tensions emerge where governors and headteachers have conflicting views on value issues, such as equal opportunities (Mahony and Riley, 1995), or when governors take the view that they are the Board of Directors of the school[9].

Peter Ribbins has argued that headteachers and governors share dual responsibility for the management of the school, an arrangement which assumes high degrees of consensus on both policy and practice (Ribbins, 1989). But how this management responsibility is divided is a source of tension. Headteachers are responsible for the educational leadership, management and organization of schools but governors can be called to account not only for any financial mismanagement in the school but for any failure of educational leadership. The management dilemma is clearly a source of concern for headteachers. Gerald Grace found that some headteachers (albeit a minority) in his study on school leadership were beginning to report problems with 'interfering governors', particularly around the issue of management (Grace, 1995). According to a national study of some 1,200 schools in England and Wales carried out in 1996, only one in three headteachers believed that the increase in the powers of school governors had improved management, and four out of five were of the view that the role of governors had to be more clearly defined (TES, 1996a).

Things are equally difficult from the governors' perspective. What one governor may perceive as an interest in a school's well-being and performance, may be defined by the headteacher as an example of governor interference. Over recent years, governors have increasingly found themselves caught between competing forces and struggling with issues of accountability and teacher professionalism. At Manton Junior School, Nottinghamshire in 1996 for example, as was discussed in the previous chapter, a bitter disagreement pitted teachers against the governors. The dispute erupted when a governors' panel decided to reinstate a boy who had been suspended for alleged bullying. Staff vigorously opposed this decision and threatened industrial action. Governors responded by setting up individual tuition for the boy, a decision which in its turn upset a number of parents who then picketed the school in protest.

On a number of other occasions, LEAs have found themselves in the middle of similar, if not quite as public, struggles, with governors asking for support to help them in dealing with headteachers who are 'under performing' (in their terms and possibly also those of Ofsted and the LEA) and headteachers complaining of the excessive demands of governors (Riley, Johnson and Rowles, 1995). Grant-maintained schools have faced similar difficulties and, in response to concerns that GM school governors have acquired too much power, GM governing bodies will be required to appoint an independent member to appeals panels where headteachers face the threat of dismissal (TES, 1996b). Given these pressures, it is not surprising that school governorships are becoming harder to fill. A national survey of some 500 schools in England and Wales carried out in 1993–94 found that one-third of governing bodies had one or more vacancies, and that recruitment difficulties were more likely to be found in inner city schools and those with a high percentage of pupils entitled to free school meals (Earley, 1994).

Relationships between headteachers and governors (and in particular the headteacher and chair of governors) range from an uneasy truce at one end of the spectrum, to a firm and consolidated school partnership at the other. Increased professional demands on heads to raise the performance of staff is likely to strengthen the leadership role of the headteacher. At the same time, the role of governors will be sharpened by the increased reliance which headteachers place on them to take on wider battles on the behalf of the school.

But can these tensions in school governance be reconciled, or indeed should they? Perhaps a degree of tension or challenge is healthy. Teachers and headteachers are not always in the right, as Tyndale has shown. Professionals will always be uneasy if their judgments are questioned by lay people. Schools have historically excluded parents. 'No parents beyond this point' was something that Plowden quite rightly challenged. Schools, even today, rarely think of parents as co-educators, an issue discussed more fully in Chapter 9.

We need to reconsider the governing body as the voice of parents and the community. Peter Newsam has suggested that the roles of governors revolve around issues of support, accountability and mediation. Firstly, governors are directly a part of the school, helping its management in particular ways, such as through oversight of finance. Secondly, they are semi-detached from the school, supporting it when required. In their role as semi-detached supporters of the school, governors are potentially an important group. As Peter Newsam concluded, 'When they act collectively, they can be an increasingly powerful and well-informed influence in support of the public education system'. Thirdly, they are the body to which the staff is accountable (Newsam, 1994, quoted in Riley with Rowles, 1997c). It is in reconciling these roles that tensions emerge.

The governing body is uniquely placed as a forum for accountability because it is both within the school and outside of it. It can work to find ways of enabling parents to engage in what is going on within the school. In particular, it can help the school to obtain a measure of the parental and community view of the school. The governing body should be more than the supporters' club and act as the school's 'critical friend', providing a healthy challenge and helping it define its aims and objectives. Where there are misunderstandings, or unhappiness about decisions which the school has taken, the governors may be able to play an important mediation role.

But if the governing body is engaged in managing and supporting schools, then tensions emerge about accountability: who is accountable to whom, and for what? Are staff accountable to the governing body for school performance, or is the governing body itself accountable to a wider community? If so, governors will need to find ways of enabling parents to engage in what is going on within the school and to locate the school within the broader community framework. The issue of account-ability becomes particularly complex in looking at curriculum issues. Governors are responsible in law for ensuring that the National Curriculum is taught, although they have no say in the content, except for particular areas such as sex education. If governors are representatives of the parents and local community, should they not be given some opportunities to have a say in curriculum priorities?

On a visit to schools in Denmark, I spent some time with members of one school board. I was particularly interested in the comments from one board member, 'Leisa'. According to her account and that of others, she had been able to persuade the board to allocate more teaching time to project work for older students which had provided them with the scope to explore complex issues in depth. She had supported the policy of ensuring that all classes were taught by both female and male teachers as a way of creating positive role models. She had also been able to feed into the school board, the views of students about spending priorities and future developments within the school.

'Leisa' was 16 years old, one of two student representatives on the school board, elected to that position by her fellow students of the Student Council, in the all-age, six-to-sixteen school. In thinking of the governing body as the voice of parents, perhaps we could also try and extend its voice to include that of students. Enabling students to have their say in determining priorities has the advantage of enabling the school to gain a full picture of what is going on. It also engages young people in solving some of the problems within their school and enables them to be seen as participants, rather than passengers in the education system.

Can School Governance be Made to Work: Can the Irreconcilable be Reconciled?

When interviewing headteachers and governors about their views of their local LEA, we asked them to define what they meant by the LEA (see Note 4). Some said it was officers, others officers and councillors, others still — officers, councillors and schools. The group who defined the LEA as being all three — 'the LEA is us, not them' — argued that the LEA existed as a broad entity because priorities were shared, and an effective and challenging dialogue existed in the locality. The embodiment of the LEA as the collective views of the locality is an ideal and the reality is likely to be far more complex. Perceptions of, and the reality of, the relationship between the LEA and schools and between headteachers and governors, form an important part of the delicate framework of school governance.

At its most basic, school governance is a political struggle about 'who gets what, when, and how' (Lasswell, 1936). It is about reconciling power and authority with autonomy and self-regulation, with the aspirations of different players, and it is about choices. We 'know' that some individuals are more powerful than others and that their power can stem from a range of sources: organizational or individual. We 'know' that power can be and is used in different ways. But in making sense of school governance and making it work, those involved also need to 'know' about the less visible and intangible dimensions of power — the collective forces and social arrangements which need to be understood if conflict is to be averted; the beliefs and preferences of individuals; and how those individuals can be brought to act together in ways that may be counter to their individual interests (Lukes, 1974). The management of school governance is a profoundly political act.

School governance is not just about overlapping spheres of authority but about zones of influence. For school governance to work effectively, some adjustments will need to be made in the relationships between all of the different parties. One aspect of the authority of the LEA stems from the legitimacy it derives from being an elected body. Its influence — in shaping thinking, in taking schools forward in a particular direction — is exercised through the nature of its leadership and is dependent on the LEA being an effective authority in the terms already described in this chapter. If the LEA is to be the protector of children's rights and the advocate for the local community — able to intervene within clearly defined boundaries — then it will need both electoral and professional legitimacy.

The authority of governors stems from their legal powers but their influence is dependent on their capacity to reflect and represent the views, attitudes and perceptions of the wider school community. If governors are to be the forum for accountability in the school, then steps need to be taken to strengthen their role as the parent, pupil and community voice.

Headteachers have considerable powers but their ability to influence the professional expertise of staff and the direction of the school is derived from their capacity to be the leading professional in the school and to be a skilful political leader, as is discussed in the next chapter. If schools are to reconcile the freedom which their new autonomy gives them, with a recognition that isolation can also stultify growth and development, then every step needs to be taken to to harness the energy, creativity and capacity for self-renewal which lies within our schools.

Notes

1 The analysis presented here is reported more fully in Riley and Rowles (1997b) which also discusses the impact of Ofsted inspection.

2 John Gray and Brian Wilcox argue that despite these difficulties, by the early 1990s, a number of LEAs were already working to put measures in place that would help them and schools assess the quality of schooling (Gray and Wilcox, 1994).

3 In 1997, Peter Wilby argued that the 'low-water mark' for LEAs had passed for two reasons. Firstly, there was the realization that the competitive market had as many weaknesses as the 'old bureaucratized professional control' — 'free-for-all admissions', for example, had not raised standards but had reinforced differences between schools. Secondly, a centralized inspectorate had proved to be an inadequate model for raising standards (Wilby, 1997b).

4 The study is being conducted by Roehampton Institute (Kathryn Riley, Jim Docking, David Rowles with support from Ian Monk). It examines the changing role and effectiveness of local education authorities. The primary focus of the study is on the relationship between the LEA and schools and the study examines the ways in which authorities set about achieving their objectives. It also examines the educational leadership of the authority, seeking to characterize what this means and how vision is translated into policy, priority and concrete action. The study is being conducted in three overlapping phases. Phase I of the project comprised a detailed case study of two London local authorities which was carried out in 1995–96. Phase II of the project was a survey of a further nine London authorities which was carried out in 1996–97. Phase III (1997–98) comprises five case studies of contrasting LEAs from different parts of England.

5 The political and value choices mediated by LEAs have been explored by Philippa Cordingley and Maurice Kogan (Cordingley and Kogan, 1993).

6 The issues presented in this section draw heavily on Riley with Rowles (1997c).

7 Frank Allen, chair of governors of a school in Cambridgeshire, has argued that Government attempts to push through contentious policies, whilst at the same time attempting to eliminate local accountability through LEAs, have in fact served to politicize governors and create a new local consensus and political force (Allen, 1995).

8 There is some evidence to suggest, however, that the inspection process, particularly the post-inspection action-plan (which must involve governors), is encouraging governing bodies to have to be clearer about their role (Earley, Fidler and Ouston, 1996).

9 Rosemary Deem has argued that some governors have interpreted this role as being comparable to that of a Board of Directors, setting clear financial targets and parameters for the performance of the headteacher whose job is envisaged as the chief executive of the organization (Deem, 1993).

Chapter 8

Whose School — The Headteacher's?

> The organization of the school must be kept mobile to its inner life.
> To one who is accustomed to wind up the machine and trust it to run
> for fixed periods, this constantly shifting shape of things will seem
> unsafe and troublesome. And troublesome it is; for no fixed plan can
> be followed; no two schools are alike; and the same school is shifting,
> requiring constant attention and nimble judgement on the part of the
> (school leader). Arnold Tomkins, education pioneer New York State,
> 1895 (Quoted in Louis, Kruse and associates, 1995, p. x)

Arnold Tomkins' assumption that the school leader has to be 'nimble
of judgment' is as true today as it was 100 years ago. What has changed,
however, is the scale and scope of the areas in which those judgments
are exercised. Only a decade and a half-ago, a Canadian study found that
a minority of elementary school principals were involved in attempting
to improve their schools' 'instructional effectiveness'. This was simply
not the task they had been set, or set themselves. The job of the school
principal in Canada, as in many other countries including the UK, was
to maintain a smooth-running organization and harmonious staff relationships. Schools functioned in the belief that teachers were competent
and needed to be left alone to teach (Leithwood and Montgomery, 1982).

Such assumptions about school principals and teachers have been
challenged over recent years. For good and ill, the job of school principal now extends far beyond maintaining good relationships within the
school. For good and ill, teachers are not left alone to teach. Our thinking about education systems and schools has also changed in many other
ways. Governments in many countries have taken a closer interest in
what goes on in schools.

In the UK, national government has been instrumental in changing expectations and introducing new structural arrangements. Financial delegation, formal accountability mechanisms and new forms of
governance have all taken their place alongside market-mechanisms
and consumer choice. Attention has also focused on the functions of
the major 'players' (headteachers, governors and, to a lesser extent, local
authorities) in achieving structural reforms. In the case of governors, the

emphasis has largely been on the legal and financial tasks and in that of headteachers, on new curriculum, financial and managerial responsibilities. The national preoccupation with structures has meant that, until recently, the significance of how school leadership is undertaken, or who undertakes it, has been underplayed, and the opportunities for parents and children to have a voice in what happens in schools largely forgotten.

Schools have increasingly been assigned the task of 'righting' a range of social and economic ills. Governments around the world have shared the belief that the macro-problems of the state and society can be addressed through improving the micro-efficiency of the school. Rising national expectations about schools have been accompanied by reduced teacher autonomy and increasing demands. At the same time, headteachers have found themselves, to a greater or lesser degree, at the centre of the debate about who governs schools and what kind of schools we want. Whilst their powers and responsibilities have grown, so too have the accountability demands.

This chapter focuses on the headteacher because much of our thinking about schools is closely tied to the person who 'heads' them. I want to look at roles, rather than functions, professional and political aspects of leadership, and to suggest that one of the major leadership challenges is to reinvigorate teachers and create a new spirit of professionalism. The speed and the manner in which many changes have been introduced over recent years have created 'change fatigue' and undermined the confidence which teachers have about themselves as professionals. As one teacher put it to me in an interview:

> So much of the time I am reacting to the agendas set by others. I never seem to have the time to catch breath and to think about what I am doing, why I am doing it, and whether I could do it better.[1]

The Nature of School Leadership

The influence of the headteacher is critical in creating the climate of a school. The actions that educational leaders take to shape, to influence and to inform their organizations will affect both the processes of schooling (the shared learning and development experience of pupils and teachers) and the outcomes (how young people feel about themselves and how equipped they are to face the challenges of adulthood). Parents, policy-makers, researchers and pupils all agree that headteachers make a difference.

But educational leadership is also something beyond the 'heroic' undertakings of one individual. Good leadership is not only shared amongst the senior management grouping but, in a healthy organization, many staff will take on important leadership roles in the life of the school. We need to see leadership not only as an aspiration of those at the top of an organization, but as something which permeates an organization and enables others to exercise leadership within their areas of expertise. Headteachers and school principals need to be leaders themselves and set the climate for leadership.

The language of leadership is itself ambiguous and betrays a lack of clarity or understanding about distinctive roles and functions. Headship is often seen as being synonymous with leadership, although in reality, of course, as I have already suggested, leadership may be shared, or may indeed be exercised by different people at different times. We found in an international project on school leadership that headteachers were now experiencing the ambivalence of leadership: problems and opportunities, momentum and direction, frustration and fulfilment[2]. Perhaps to some extent this has always been true, but the new element is that the conditions and demands of school leadership have changed whereas the impulse which has taken people into that role has not:

> Headteachers who want to spend time with children, on learning and teaching, or professional development find they have to give priority to external relationships, paperwork, policy and politics. This inevitably creates deep seated tensions between maintaining and developing, and between managing and leading schools. (MacBeath and Riley, 1997, p. 3)

Changing relationships and the growing expectations of various groups create new demands. Parents are now more aware of their rights, governors of their role in accountability. Students are more questioning. The boundaries of school leadership have altered considerably and headteachers now have a range of external constituents, including future 'customers'.

One of the conclusions from our project on leadership has been that constructions of leadership have become too narrow and have not taken into account sufficiently the range of contextual factors which impact on school leadership. Our understanding of leadership does not just stem from context, however, but also from a willingness to see leadership in the round and recognize its mobility and fragility. School leadership is intrinsically bound in its context (global, national, local and school-based) and constructions of 'effective leadership' are profoundly value-laden, relating to both national and school-based purposes. National constructions of leadership create differing expectations about the role of the headteacher. In Denmark, there is a strong emphasis on the internal world of the school and, in particular, the teacher's world. In Scotland, national constructions of leadership place a heavy weight on the role of the headteacher as leading professional but also emphasize the pupil world. In England, changes in governance and external forms of account-ability challenge some aspects of the autonomy of the headteacher as leading professional, whilst demanding that a balance be struck between the competing demands of the external world and a closer involvement in the internal world of the school.

The power of headteachers has undoubtedly shifted dramatically over recent years in response to a range of external pressures. The tension is in managing the 'fit': between the external world and the internal world of the school, between a sharper focus on staff and pupil performance, and classroom pedagogy. The school leader has to create the environment for school leadership which enables others to take their role. This means creating the conditions for learning for staff and pupils; respecting and enhancing staff autonomy within clear bound-aries; and leading children towards greater autonomy and independence. School leadership is about meeting and exceeding old expectations and creating new expectations in children, staff and parents.

Leadership is also shaped by the personal characteristics and ex-perience which individuals bring to the position. Gender is undoubtedly a factor because of the expectations that people hold about appro-priate behaviour for either sex and leadership styles[3,4]. We found that where there was a male headteacher and female deputy, a 'work-wife' situation sometimes emerged in which the woman (deputy) took on a substantial amount of the business of taking care of relationships. We also found some evidence that the job of headship is increasingly being seen seen by governors as 'men's business', requiring skills (financial and managerial) and abilities (to control 'miscreants') which men were deemed more likely than women to hold (Mahony and Riley, 1995).

The question put to headteachers in our school leadership project — 'Whose expectations count?' — brought no simple answers, as they tried to weigh the demands, and the legitimacy of the demands, from different constituents. The school leader must be able to 'read' the con-text and pull together all the perceptions of the various interest groups. Our analysis also suggests that in order to deal with the complexities of leadership, headteachers need to adapt a repertoire of management styles. As one headteacher put it, 'In the past headteachers could adopt one management style which they polished to perfection'. This is no longer the case. Headteachers and school principals need to be able to lead and manage in both 'hard' and 'soft' domains, as leadership is mani-fested through cohesion and consensus, as well as through conflict.

Demands on time, differing expectations, and competition among priorities were all potential ingredients of conflict. Conflict existed in a number of spheres and manifested itself in different forms. Headteachers responded to conflict in various ways as 'referee', 'player', or 'torch bearer', in other words, acting as neutral arbiter, becoming involved, or using the conflict to forge principles and policy. As the 'referee', head-teachers were involved in mediating conflict between and within differ-ent groups: parents, staff and students. At its most extreme, mediating conflict involved breaking up a fight between staff, or between parents. Even where the examples are less dramatic, managing conflict is not easy.

Where the headteacher is acting as a 'player,' she or he is directly involved in issues which can have a profound effect on people's lives such as promotion or redundancy, pupil exclusions, disciplinary proce-dures in relation to staff. For many headteachers, this involvement is at great personal cost and is often a source of loneliness and isolation. In the final role as 'torch bearer', headteachers have to deal with the con-flict which emerges when they pursue deeply held values about equality and social justice, which may challenge the prejudices of individuals or groups. As 'torch bearer' the headteacher knowingly embarks on a course of action which may create conflict in order to pursue important value objectives.

The school is an intensely political organization and conflict is one aspect of the micro-politics but there are many other elements. Stephen Ball has linked elements in the external environment to the policy processes (Ball, 1987). Andy Hargreaves has focused on central organizational elements such as collegiality — genuine, or contrived — (Hargreaves, 1991). Hugh Busher and Rene Saran have identified both formal and informal power structures (Busher and Saran, 1994). A focus on the micro-politics reinforces the importance of the political leader-ship skills of the headteacher.

The Headteacher as 'Political' Leader

I use the term political leadership because the headteacher of today is expected to be a significant player in a whole galaxy of sometimes separate, sometimes interlocking spheres: governing bodies, local au-thorities, central government, parents, teacher unions and, of course, the school itself — teachers and students. Regardless of whether rela-tionships are antagonistic or consensual, those groups will inevitably have different and competing interests and expectations. One critical aspect of the headteacher's role is to manage those differences — a task requiring immense political skills.

There is a curiously British aversion to talking about the political skills needed for leadership. The development of political skills is seen as synonymous with gamesmanship. It is politicians who use political skills and 'politics' is something slightly tainted. Such avoidance tactics enable public servants to let themselves off the hook, free to play the part of the political innocent. Effective headteachers, as others in senior leadership roles, have always exercised 'political' skills, seeking alliances (largely with staff); deciding on courses of action about the fate of individuals (the suspension of a child, for example); and drawing on their own beliefs and judgments in order to make decisions about the use of resources (the allocation of staff time to particular groups of children). They have always had considerable scope to exercise their discretion — an essentially value-based activity (Manley-Casimir, 1991).

The nature of the political leadership of a school is bound in context. Danish school leaders in our project on school leadership did not see themselves as operating politically, or in a political context. Scottish and English heads were more likely to see the internal organization as a political arena, and English heads were most likely of all to see their job as political in dealing with the larger community, and large 'p' political in opposing, or supporting national government reform. English headteachers have, with much political resistance, been 'empowered' by government legislation. This has placed on them a much greater burden of accountability, a reduced financial base and a new market vulnerability. But it has also given them greater freedom and flexibility to run their own schools. 'My school' and 'my staff' are everyday phrases among headteachers. Such proprietorial language is not new, of course. Current reforms have simply built upon a long-standing tradition (most notably in the independent sector) in which the headteacher was virtually synonymous with the school.

Simon Baddeley and Kim James (1987) have explored political leadership from the perspective of the skills needed by senior managers in the public sector. They suggest that managers need to be able to operate on two dimensions, the 'reading' dimension and the 'carrying' dimension. The 'reading' dimension requires the manager to develop his or her capacity to recognize patterns, to draw on past experience and to note the unique elements of a situation: an activity described by one headteacher in the project on effective leadership as the ability to 'read the runes'. Baddeley describes it in the following terms:

> Reading' refers to our feel for the political context, objects and institutions around us and the purposes they represent. (Baddeley, 1992, p. 6)

The second dimension is the 'carrying' dimension: the feelings, thoughts and predispositions which an individual brings to a situation. At the positive end of the 'carrying' dimension is behaviour which is based on learning and integrity: an attempt to marry the inner world and the needs of the self with the outer world — the needs of others. At the negative end of the 'carrying' dimension is an aversion to learning and a propensity to games playing.

While being good or bad at 'reading' has no moral connotations, the inability of a headteacher to 'read' fluently must create serious institutional weaknesses. A politically inept leader who has no understanding of power and who has little idea about how to act skilfully and with integrity can damage a school. This damage can not be compensated by the headteacher's profound understanding of the curriculum, or deep commitment to children. The mantle of wilful innocence feigned is a comfortable position but one which ultimately, if assumed by the headteacher, can jeopardize important educational goals. The headteacher is central to the political processes[5,6].

In managing the political process, the headteacher or school principal faces a range of dilemmas. Joe Murphy has described these as fourfold: the complexity dilemma, the search dilemma, the dilemma of self and the accountability dilemma. The complexity dilemma emerges because principals have become so overwhelmed by the expectations of reform. Work overload, lack of trust and competing expectations mean that headteachers are often caught between conflicting forces. The search dilemma signals the confusions for principals in finding the road ahead through the complexities of reform, with little support provided for them in carrying out these varying tasks. The dilemma of self reflects the struggle that school principals have in trying to get a sense of their emerging role. Principals need to relinquish previous roles but this process of abandonment is not without costs. Finally, the accountability dilemma reflects the particular tension for the school principal in trying to involve others in school governance whilst at the same time also being the person who ultimately takes responsibility when things go wrong (Murphy, 1994, pp. 39–46)[7].

To whom, and how are headteachers accountable for their performance and that of the school? There is accountability to central government, through external inspection and national tests, and accountability to local education authorities (which is somewhat ill-defined). There is accountability to parents (although this is particularly loosely expressed), and there is specific accountability to governors. Political leadership is an essential attribute if headteachers are to be able to respond to the complex accountability agenda. Being a 'wise' political

117

leader, however, is not an alternative to being a professional leader. Both are needed.

Creating a Professional Community

As the professional leader of the school, the school principal, or head-teacher, needs to create a professional community of learners. But when we think about learning, we tend to see that as something that pupils do but not teachers. Yet teachers need to be learners too, constantly reflecting and developing. Teachers' learning is enhanced where there is a climate of trust; where their learning is focused and orientated towards solving the sorts of problems which individual pupils face; and where opportunities for teachers to work together are positively encouraged.

Findings from an American study suggest that schools which are professional school communities are characterized by a number of common features. These include shared values, reflective dialogue, 'de-privatization' of practice (i.e. the sharing of professional understandings), a focus on student learning, and collaboration. In building up a professional community, school leaders need to take into account a broad range of contextual variables: the commitment, experience, expectations and expertise of the staff; the school resources; student intake and physical environment; as well as their own personal characteristics and local and national factors (Louis et al., 1995). The task is to create a climate of learning and enquiry which is characterized by openness, and in which mentoring, co-teaching, classroom observation and feedback by peers, and discussions about pedagogy and curriculum are the norm. Teachers need to be drawn into a professional community and away from their isolation. As part of such a community they will also enjoy a large degree of autonomy.

Successful organizations are those in which all the players are involved in decision-making, and there is considerable evidence to suggest that teachers are more likely to be drawn into making changes within their own schools when a more open, collaborative leadership climate prevails:

> ... Teachers' willingness to participate in school decision-making is influenced primarily by their relationships with their principals ... Teachers appear more willing to participate in all areas of decision-making if they perceive their relationships with their principals as more open, collaborative, facilitative and supportive. They are less willing to participate in any decision-making if they characterize their relationships with the principals as closed, exclusionary, and controlling. (Smylie, 1992, p. 63; quoted in Murphy, 1994, p. 30)

Encouraging teachers to be involved in change and to take on new responsibilities, including the responsibility for their own development, creates the foundations for a professional community but this 'recasting' will not in itself improve student performance (Elmore, 1993). The changes and the refocusing must be directly linked to expectations about students, to student attitudes about themselves, to what goes on in classrooms on a daily basis, and to student achievement[8].

Headteachers' credibility as professional leaders largely derives from their ability to create an open climate, a participative decision-making culture in which pupil interests are placed at the centre[9]. This analysis has been reinforced by findings from an OECD study of 11 countries (including the UK) which looked at teacher quality. The study concluded that teacher quality was influenced by a range of factors which included the individual qualities which teachers brought to their job, and the conditions in particular schools and the national context (OECD, 1994). Schools that exhibited unusually high levels of teacher quality had the following characteristics:

- a clear vision or moral purpose;
- a commitment to collaborative teacher development;
- an investment in high quality teachers as part of recruitment and staff development and an encouragement of 'risk-taking' school leadership at all levels of the school;
- a management infrastructure which supported high quality teaching and learning and the use of teams, informal networks, involvement in decision-making; and
- a symbiotic relationship between the school, its district authority and community (which involved) pressure and support at all levels within the context of shared educational values (a notion which expresses the nature of the ideal school–LEA partnership described in the previous chapter). (ibid. p. 112)

Leadership of a professional community has opportunities as well as pitfalls. The headteacher has to stimulate a climate of professional debate and challenge, but equally, 'avoiding confrontation between staff who cherish different values seems to be as important as constructing a global consensus' (Busher and Saran, 1994, p. 6) a lesson which Terry Ellis would have done well to learn[10]. Good leaders are themselves learners. School teachers in Canada rated school principals as effective if they worked hard; had lots of energy; were genuine in their beliefs; modelled openness and had good people skills; and, most importantly, showed evidence of learning by growing and changing themselves

(Leithwood et al., 1997). Good schools are sailed rather than driven (Hopkins, 1992).

Voices at Two Ends of the Spectrum

Concern about how schools are led and managed has led to a search for the essential features of school leadership, and to the establishment of basic standards for school leaders. In England and Wales, a National Professional Qualification for Headship (NPQH) for aspiring head-teachers is being introduced by the Teacher Training Agency (TTA) and is likely to become a mandatory requirement for headship selection. The TTA is also setting national standards for teachers at all stages of their professional life as a way of enhancing their professional status, creating development opportunities and improving the quality of teaching.

The TTA describes the core purposes of headship as providing 'professional leadership for a school which secures its success and improvement, ensuring high quality education for all its pupils and improved standards of learning and achievement' (TTA, 1997, p. 1). Similarly, the US Consortium of Chief State School Officers has produced standards for school leaders as a point of 'leverage' in the system. Each of the six standards begins with the core statement, 'A school administrator is an educational leader who promotes the success of all students by . . .

- facilitating the development, articulation, implementation and stewardship of a vision of learning that is shared and supported by the local community;
- advocating, nurturing, and sustaining a school culture and instructional program conducive to student learning and staff professional development;
- ensuring management of the organization, operations, and resources for a safe, efficient and effective learning environment;
- collaborating with families and community learning members, responding to diverse community interests and needs, and mobilizing community resources;
- acting with integrity, fairness, and in an ethical manner;
- understanding, responding to, and influencing the larger political, social, economic legal and cultural context. (CCSSO, 1996, pp. 7–18)

Both sets of standards emphasize the importance of the school leader in creating and sustaining a vision. The notion of 'stewardship' expressed in the American proposals is an interesting one and suggests that the school leader's role is to look after the well-being of the school on behalf of others, both within the school and the local education community. 'Acting with integrity, fairness, and in an ethical manner' is akin to the concept of 'wise' political leadership skills described earlier in the chapter.

To meet the challenges of the future, school leaders will (according to the US Chief State School Officers) require a 'portfolio' of skills. They envisage a future in which teaching and learning will be redefined and previous assumptions about the school as a bureaucratic and hierarchical organization will be challenged by notions of the school as a community. The role of a range of stakeholders external to the school will grow in significance. Views about schools, what they are for, and how they should be led and managed will also change radically.

It seems right that national standards of expectations should be set for school leaders. What these standards are, and whether they can be measured as competencies is, however, a complex issue but I want here to bring a different perspective into the debate about school leaders — that of children. They remind us how crucial is the contribution that the headteacher can make to creating a climate of respect in which people can live, as well as learn together.

Through our work on school leadership, we have been able to gain some understanding of what children think about their school leaders. The children we worked with in our project were very clear about what really matters in schools. In answer to the question 'What is a headteacher?' English children thought that the headteacher 'holds the school in her hands'. On a more mundane basis, the headteacher was the person who provided everything from pencils and books to 'hooks to hang our coats on'.

The headteacher 'walks around the school to make sure that people treat each other nicely' and attends lots of meetings. Safety and security were important, 'She makes sure that the gates are locked and we are safe', as well as ensuring that the school is a pleasant place to be. 'He says good morning to my mum', commented one six year old. 'The head gives us laughter and makes joy in the school', wrote another six year old in a wonderful accolade to that particular headteacher. The headteacher has to be firm and fair but also needs to have 'a soft spot'. According to these children, the headteacher undoubtedly influences the school climate and environment in significant ways.

Children think you become a head 'by taking an exam in kindness', by 'buying a school', 'by reading a book about it', 'by going to a school and seeing whether you like children' or, 'by years of hard work and kindness'. With some prescience one thought, 'the Government lets you' become a head. One group of nine year olds worked with me to construct a job description for a headteacher.

Qualification for Headteachers: 'An Exam in Kindness'

In order to become a headteacher you must:

- Have a good education and be able to solve problems
- Be very experienced as a teacher
- Be able to understand children (what they can do at different ages)
- Be easy going but firm
- Know how to look after the building (create a nice environment and a safe place for children)
- Know how to take responsibility for things happening in the school and not blame others
- Be able to make children, adults and the community confident about the things they do in school
- Provide a good example in your behaviour (by not smoking, or drinking in school)
- Not be racist and make others see that the colour of your skin does not matter
- Keep in touch with the local community, letting them know what is happening in the school
- Treat children equally
- Give everyone the same advantages

Having written the job description, the children then wrote the accompanying advert:

Headteacher Wanted

Come to 'our' school. It is a good school. The teachers are good, the children will welcome you and everyone will treat you well.

If you are going to apply for this job, you will have to be able to communicate with children, be respectful of them and understand their point of view. You will need to be well qualified and experienced.

You will need to be energetic, outgoing, confident, mix with people easily and understand their feelings. You will need to be able to understand other people's beliefs and be a calming influence on the school.

Try your luck and be the best!

Notes

1 This interview took place in 1997 as part of a project on the development of leadership teams in schools, undertaken with colleagues at the Roehampton Institute.

2 The International project, 'Effective Leadership in a Time of Change', involves researchers from the Roehampton Institute, London (Kathryn Riley and Pat Mahony), the University of Strathclyde (John MacBeath, Jenny Reeves and Joan Forrest), the Royal Danish School of Educational Studies (Chresten Kruchov, Lejf Moos and Johnny Thomassen) and Griffith University, Queensland (Neil Dempster and Lloyd Logan). Findings from the project will be published in 1998.

3 Research on leadership has demonstrated that the road to leadership is frequently different for women and men. There is evidence that men are encouraged to apply for senior posts at an earlier stage in their career and are given more opportunities to experience leadership (Leithwood, Steinbach and Begley, 1991). Women are more likely than men to have encountered particular barriers in their career development (Hill and Ragland, 1995). Transnationally, there is also evidence to suggest that women's career paths are predicated on their role within the family (Davies, 1990). Analysis has also highlighted the under representation of women at senior managerial levels in education and the decline of women in teaching as the age of the students rise (Riley, 1994c, p. 88).

4 The issue of gender and leadership style is one which I have pursued more fully elsewhere (Riley, 1994c) and will be developed in the forthcoming book on the school leadership project. One of the issues is the extent to which women's leadership style is different to that of men. American writer Judy Rosener (1990) has argued that because of their socialization, women are more likely to have adopted more participatory and inclusive styles than their male peers. This was certainly the perception of many of the headteachers in our leadership project (both female and male).

5 This assertion is reinforced by findings from a comprehensive review of the changing role of leadership in restructuring schools which identifies micro-politics as being central to effective school restructuring and as being largely managed by the school leadership (Murphy and Louis, 1994).

6 Rational choice theory which starts from a belief that politics is a contest about particular outcomes, and involves strategies, tactics, gamesmanship, bargaining and coalitions has been used as one way of trying to explain these complexities. Rational choice theory assumes that 'all political actors — voters, professional politicians, bureaucrats — have preferences and make rationally calculated choices to maximize the realization of their preferences at the least cost' (Boyd, Crowson and van Geel, 1994, p. 129).

7 The tensions and dilemmas are evident in the images which headteachers have about themselves. See Kruchov, MacBeath and Riley (1996) for illustration of this.

8 A closer link needs to be made between development planning, classroom practice and pupil learning (Stoll and Fink, 1992).

9 The headteacher needs to develop collaborative if not collegial ways of working (Hargreaves, 1991; Huberman, 1993). Collaboration and collegiality are not the same and David Hargreaves has argued that 'collaboration is possible in both traditional and collegial cultures'. However, 'in most circumstances collegial cultures should favour the self-improving school' (Hargreaves, 1995, pp. 42–3). Collegiality is not a goal in its own right. It needs to be linked to notions of organizational learning and improvement of student performance.

10 Headteachers in our study on school leadership argued that the headteacher needed to create collaboration and greater openness, but in order to achieve this in secondary schools they might well need to challenge 'the subject barons' (that is the heads of department).

Chapter 9

Whose School — Teachers', Pupils' or Parents'?

I was supposed to be a welfare statistic . . . It is because of a teacher that I sit at this table. I remember her telling us one cold, miserable day that she could not make our clothing better; she could not provide us with food; she could not change the terrible segregated conditions under which we lived. She could introduce us to the world of reading, the world of books and that is what she did.

What a world! I visited Asia and Africa. I saw magnificent sunsets; I tasted exotic foods; I fell in love and danced in wonderful halls. I ran away with escaped slaves and stood besides a teenage martyr. I visited lakes and streams and composed lines of verse. I knew then that I wanted to help children do the same things, I wanted to weave magic . . . New York Teacher (Evidence submitted to 'The National Commission on Teaching and America's Future', 1996, p. iii)

At the end of the last chapter we heard children's views about the important qualities of headship. It is rare that children's voices are heard in educational debates[1]. Schools, Jean Ruddock has argued, do not listen to what children say. There is the popular annual ritual of publishing 'howlers' from examination scripts — 'The first women to vote were called the Suffer Jets'. 'A rhetorical question is a question there is no answer to, like: What has this government been doing since it came to power?' Children are involved in discussions about particular aspects of school life, but there is a reluctance to take seriously young people's critique of education, or their perceptions of it because of tradition and teacher anxiety (Ruddock, 1996, pp. 2–3).

Listening to children's voices smacks of the progressive traditions in education which have been derided over recent years — Plowden, Rousseau, William Blake, Mary Wollstonecraft, Dora Russell. The extent and ways in which schools listen to children reflect deep-seated assumptions about teachers and taught. If childhood is seen as a passive state, then in the tradition of Locke, children will need to be 'formed' by instruction. Their views about their educational experience will be of little consequence. If, however, as I have argued, children and young people are considered to be active learners, then schools will want to engage them in the learning partnership. Children have much to learn, much to be taught, but they are not empty vessels and they also have much to give. Their voices deserve to be listened to and they can make a significant contribution to creating a vibrant school community of learners which includes teachers, as well as pupils.

Some years ago, I looked at race and gender issues in schools in South London: how the pupils themselves viewed the quality of their educational experience and how individual teachers and particular schools could offer very different experiences to young people from similar backgrounds (Riley, 1994c). Some had been inspired by their teachers, as the New York teacher quoted in the opening paragraphs of this chapter. Some had been marginalized by their school experience, black girls made 'invisible', white girls overshadowed in male dominated schools. But what struck me at the time and since was both how accurate they were in their assessments of the schools and the teachers, how clear they were about what needed to be improved, and how understanding they were of the pressures which their teachers faced.

What Kinds of Teachers, for What Kinds of Job?[2]

Over recent years, governments of the day have come to perceive teachers as part of the educational problem. The national climate of blaming and shaming which prevailed for a number of years, and which continued in the immediate post-election period, undoubtedly contributed to the fall in students wishing to train as teachers in 1997 (Guardian, 1997b). Teacher supply is influenced — positively and negatively — by national expectations and attitudes towards teachers.

In France, the Government announces annually the number of teacher vacancies which are likely to be available for the following year. In 1997, the figure was 25,000 and some 200,000 graduate students sat the test, success in which would enable them to embark upon a twelve month teacher training programme at one of France's 29 education institutions, before taking up a teaching post. To enhance their chances of passing that test, many of the students will have already completed a one year preliminary teacher training course. In Scotland there are now ten applicants for every one teacher training place and there are no subject shortages.

Twenty-two miles divide England from France. In England, there are major problems of recruitment of students to train as teachers, there are acute shortages of trained teachers in particular areas (particularly mathematics and science) and there are problems of retention of both junior and experienced staff[3]. What makes teaching a more attractive proposition in France, or Scotland, than in England? The most obvious reasons are that French teachers are relatively well paid, teaching has some status in French society, and once they have passed fairly stringent tests of proficiency, French teachers, compared with their English counterparts, enjoy a large degree of professional autonomy. Scottish teachers also enjoy a higher status than their English counterparts and, according to Ivor Sutherland, Rector (Chief Executive) of the Scottish General Teaching Council, morale is higher in Scotland because 'teachers haven't had quite the same bashing as the profession South of the border' (TES, 1997b, p. 3).

We have witnessed growing demands and expectations on teachers over recent years and greater demands for accountability. There has also been a growing trend towards the introduction of national and state standards and accreditation. At the same time, there has been a debate about the nature of teaching as a profession. Lee Shulman has described these developments in the following terms:

> Most of the current reforms rest on the call for greater professionalization in teaching, with higher standards for entry, greater emphasis on the scholarly bases for practice, more rigorous programs of theoretical and practical preparation, better strategies for certification and licensure . . . In large measure they call for teaching to follow the model of other professions that define their knowledge bases in systematic terms, require extended periods of preparation, socialize neophytes into practice with extended periods of internship and residency, and imply demanding national and state certification procedures. (Shulman, 1987, p. 20)

Lee Shulman also goes on to suggest, however, that in the US these changes have been accompanied by parallel shifts in the workplace that have permitted greater autonomy and teacher leadership. This has not been the case in England. A strong accountability framework has been established, new methods of accreditation and national standards have been, and are being developed, but concepts of trust and authority have been challenged, if not eroded.

Proposals to set up a General Teaching Council (GTC) in England by the year 2000 bring some of the essential elements of the debate about the nature of teaching as profession to the fore. If society is to trust its professionals, then it needs to be convinced that the community which represents that professional group is assuring quality. In the case of the proposed General Teaching Council for England, however, the Government intends to retain responsibility for controlling teacher quality. According to Schools' Minister Stephen Byers, the GTC will be a 'General Teaching Council not a General Teachers' Council' (Financial Times,

1997b). The new advisory body is not designed to be a self-regulating body of the teaching profession unlike the General Medical Council or the Bar Council.

Nevertheless, ministers launching the proposals have suggested that the new GTC will have a role to play in advising on the entrance requirements for new aspirants, assessing the effectiveness of the induction year of newly qualified teachers, establishing agreed standards of teacher conduct and barring incompetent teachers. However, teachers will be in a minority and the GTC will be made up of representatives of business, local authorities, parents and school governors. Teacher unions will not have direct representation on the Council. The English GTC will have considerably less clout and autonomy than its long established Scottish counterpart which is responsible for accrediting all initial teacher education.

The question of the structure of a GTC is only part of the debate about the nature of teaching as a profession. There is the question of how far teaching should follow the pattern of the legal or medical professions. There are also issues to do with the attributes of professions. In general, professions probably have a number of characteristics which include a concept of social purpose and social obligation, underpinned by an ethical foundation. This concept of social purpose has historically enabled groups, such as doctors, to acquire a degree of autonomy. Professions also have strong routes into a body of academic knowledge which links theory to practice, and a notion of professional practice which is characterized by the ability to draw on that knowledge base to exercise judgment and make decisions. Exercising judgment is at the centre of what it means to be a professional and implies an ability to deal with complexity and uncertainty. Professions also regulate themselves and discipline their members.

Teaching has a clear social purpose. It has strong academic links and theoretical underpinnings. Aspiring teachers are expected increasingly to demonstrate deep understandings of their specialist subject areas, but are teachers trusted to exercise their own judgment? If one of the characteristics of a profession is the scope which is given to its member to exercise their judgment, in the case of teachers this certainly has been substantially eroded.

Questions about the nature of teaching as a profession are far from new. In the closing days of the 1939–45 war, Arnold McNair was given the task by the Churchill Government of looking at the supply, recruitment and training of teachers. The McNair Report concluded that the teaching profession would need to be made more attractive and its status enhanced as:

England, — we do not say England and Wales — has never attached enough importance to education and has therefore never given the teaching profession the esteem it deserves. (McNair, quoted in Smith, 1946, p. 233)

The report argued for a change in heart and emphasized the importance of teacher quality. If the country was to create a 'wise democracy' in the post-Hitler world, then it would need to recruit people of the highest calibre to teaching. The report argued that the ban on married women teachers (which had been imposed by many local authorities) should be reversed, as it resulted in the loss of a highly qualified and dedicated group of teachers (ibid. p. 24). Teachers, it was argued, often led a narrow life, living as a 'race apart', and should be encouraged to participate in public affairs (ibid. p. 25)[4]. Teaching required more than knowledge of subject matter and involved many 'functions' and the teacher needed to be able to interpret the meaning of complex changes. A critical element of the job was to enable young people to be able to discriminate and not be 'an easy prey to sensations and cheap appeals' (McNair, quoted in Smith, 1946, p. 234). The teaching profession had a strong social purpose and was to be at the heart of the post-war reconstruction of society.

In the Tyndale aftermath, questions about the nature of teaching as a profession emerged sharply. A Marxist critique of events at Tyndale argued that the teachers at Tyndale had fallen prey to one of the besetting vices of radical teachers: a 'left professionalism' which separated them from the wider working-class community (Socialist Teacher, 1977, p. 8). Another article of the day described this quandary in the following terms:

The whole tendency of teacher organizations has been to define themselves as professionals, experts and so on; to reinforce the fact that in terms of the work that they do they are firmly distinguished from manual labour . . . Teachers and their organizations have emphasized (with fatal continuity) their professional status, the mental-manual labour divide, their distance from parentdom, and so on, so that teaching has been ideologically constructed to emphasize differences from the working class. (Finn, Grant and and Johnson, 1977, p. 180)

What is the impact of being a professional group? In boosting the status of 'professional' we may risk the danger of severing the links between professionals and those they are supposed to 'serve'. Professions have a tendency to pursue the interests of their own group which may not always coincide with those of the client, the patient or the student. There is also a danger that too much emphasis on the notion of teaching as a profession will place undue weight on the knowledge content of teaching — the foundation which underpins it — and not enough on the superstructure of the practice, the relationships with children and young people, the process of discovery and inquiry. A delicate balance needs to be struck between these differing elements. Lee Shulman describes this tension in the following terms:

> We must be careful that the knowledge base approach does not pro-
> duce an overly technical image of teaching, a scientific enterprise that
> has lost its soul. (Shulman, 1987, p. 20)

In creating a robust model of teaching as a profession for the twenty-first century, we need to draw on the strengths of the range of models of professions which already exist. But we also need to con-struct new understandings about the profession of teaching which take into account the nature of teaching and which emphasize the role of teachers as part of a professional community. The experience of 'failing' schools described in Chapter 6, reinforces the importance of this point. The schools did not see themselves as part of a wider professional com-munity and the teachers were isolated and lacked professional links or interactions (Riley and Rowles, 1997a).

Participation in such professional networks is critical if teachers are to become professionals, as is well-focused professional develop-ment[5]. Joan Talbert and Milbrey McLaughlin present evidence from an American study of some 800 teachers in California which suggests that teachers who participate in 'strong professional communities within their own subject area departments or other teacher networks have higher levels of professionalism . . . than do teachers in less collegial settings'. Such teachers have 'higher levels of shared standards for curriculum and instruction, evidence a stronger service ethic in their relations with students, and show stronger commitment to the teaching profession' (Talbert and McLaughlin, 1994, pp. 142–3).

Some countries have sought to maximize professional collabora-tion. In Japan, for example, the relative success of the Japanese school system is frequently attributed to formal teaching methods but another important element is that Japanese schools rely heavily on teacher col-laboration, and teachers are supported by cooperative management. Peer planning, rather than individual teacher planning, is the norm, and teachers attend demonstration classes within their own schools which focus on teacher-style, student interactions and modes of learning. Schools are encouraged to flourish as professional communities.[6]

National policies — which have placed schools in competition with each other for 'clients' — have worked against the creation of teaching as a professional community in England and have, according to Mike Bottery and Nigel Wright, contributed to teacher deprofessionalization. However, they also point to the failure of schools and of the teachers within them, 'to seek a deeper understanding of what being a professional entails' (Bottery and Wright, 1997, p. 22). The responsibility for creating a professional teaching community lies, therefore, with national government, with local government (as discussed in Chapter 6) and with teachers and schools themselves.

A vibrant professional community is one in which teachers are not distanced from children and their experience. In the extract from a US report on teaching quoted at the beginning of the chapter, a New York teacher explained why she had become a teacher. The teacher who had inspired her not only had a deep understanding and passion for her subject but a strong emotional commitment to her students. The classroom was not a 'barren and boring' place, as Andy Hargreaves has argued, but a 'labour of love' (Hargreaves, 1997, p. 4).

The Parent-school Partnership

If teachers are to engage in a new relationship with students, what then should be their relationship with parents, and what should be the involvement of parents in the life of the school? Views about parents and their involvement in schools have undergone a number of shifts over the last thirty years or so. In the 1960s, as discussed in Chapter 2, Plowden challenged the 'no parents beyond this point' approach of many schools. Reducing social disadvantage was a priority, and home-school links were to be encouraged, particularly those which aimed to foster 'good parenting'. In the 1970s, Tyndale brought the parental issue to the fore — what legitimacy did parents have to question the professional judgments of teachers? In the wake of Tyndale, the Taylor Committee was set up to look at school governance and recommended that parents should be given a legitimate say in the management of the school through representation on governing bodies.

According to an OECD study, many countries are beginning to think about how to develop policies which will involve parents more closely in the education of their children (OECD, 1997). The growing emphasis on the relationship between families and schools, and the search for ways of involving parents in the education process, has been driven by different and sometimes competing factors: national government and school perceptions that parents should take responsibility for their child's behaviour; growing assertions about the rights of parents to make choices about their child's education; and a belief that parents and teachers are jointly engaged in the shared activity of educating children. Parents want to be able to support their child's school education. Parental involvement is associated with higher achievement in school and in de-centralized systems governments increasingly want to make schools more accountable to their clients.

The OECD study, led by Caroline St John Brooks, looked at families and schools in Canada, Denmark, England and Wales, France, Germany, Ireland, Japan, Spain and the United States. It highlighted the relatively untapped potential of parental education in assisting parents from disadvantaged socio-economic backgrounds to support their children's learning more effectively. The study concluded that improving understanding of the educational process not only enabled parents to become more involved in the school, but could give them the confidence to continue with further education themselves. School-based initiatives to involve parents could improve equity, encourage life-long learning and help to reduce exclusion (ibid.). The latter point has been reinforced by a Canadian study on teacher-parent partnerships which found that where there was effective collaboration both pupils and parents felt a stronger bond with the school with positive consequences for all (Coleman, Collinge and Tabin, 1996).

Throughout the 1980s and 1990s, parents in England and Wales were given more rights and more specific responsibilities[7]. The nature of these responsibilities is defined in legislation and the framing of such national legislation conveys deep-seated assumptions about schools, teachers and parents. A comparison between English and Danish legislation conveys, both in tone and content, quite different relationships. The Education Act (England and Wales) 1988 may have given parents a consumer role but they, unlike parents in Denmark, are not seen as co-educators.

> It shall be the duty of the parent of every child of compulsory school age to cause him to receive full-time education suitable to his age, ability and aptitude, either by regular attendance at school or otherwise. (Education Act 1988, England and and Wales, Section 1976)

> The task of the basic school is, in co-operation with parents, to offer possibilities for the children to acquire knowledge, skills, working methods and forms of expression which contribute to the all-round development of the individual child. (Folkeskole Act of 1993, article 1.1; quoted in MacBeath, Moos and Riley, 1996, p. 226)

There are also differences in how parents themselves perceive their role in the educational process, in one country compared to another.

As part of its work on comparative data, the OECD looked at what the general public in eleven countries saw as the respective responsibilities of school and home. Asked to say whether they thought responsibility for personal and social development of young people should be the main task of home or school, overall, respondents from all eleven countries saw this as a shared obligation. However, there were wide variations between countries. Taking the three countries which were part of our study on school leadership, the majority of the general public in Denmark saw personal and social development as a responsibility of the home, whereas in Scotland and England this was viewed as a shared responsibility of the home and the school (OECD, 1995b, p. 57).

Table 1   Percentage of the general public saying how much responsibility home should have for personal and social development compared to the school

responsibility —	home	shared	school
Denmark	55	43	2
England/Wales	14	81	5
Scotland	20	78	3

Source: OECD, 1995b, quoted in MacBeath, Moos and Riley, 1996, p. 251.

Through the 1988 Act, parents were given the opportunity to choose a school for their child. But parental 'choice' was in reality the right to express a preference, and the right to appeal if that preference was not satisfied. Parents had the right to vote for grant-maintained status of their child's school but, having exercised this right through a parental ballot, ceased to have any involvement in determining how the school should function. Research on grant-maintained schools has also shown that the move towards GM status was more likely to be driven by the headteacher, or governors, than parents (Fitz, Halpin and Powers, 1993). Through the 'Parents' Charter' — which was launched by Prime Minister John Major — parents were given the right to receive information about their child's performance at school. But parents were not given any right to have a say in how their child was taught, or what they were taught (apart from the limited opportunity to 'opt out' of an act of Collective Worship, or sex education).

Parents can express their views at transition points in their child's education, or they can choose, as many did at Tyndale, to remove their child from one school and place him or her in another[8]. But exercising this right has rather more consequences than changing a brand of washing-powder. When a school closure is planned parents have few rights. They can express their views in support of, or against, closure, but they may end up being directed to send their child to an alternative school. This was the case in Hackney, where in 1995, a Government appointed Education Association recommended the closure of Hackney Downs School in London[9]. In looking at all these various facets of parental rights, the definition of the parent as 'active' consumer remains relatively weak and, on a day to day basis, 'opportunities for the exercise of the individual or collective parental voice within schools appear limited' (Vincent and Tomlinson, 1997, p. 365).

Caroline Vincent and Sally Tomlinson have argued that prevailing definitions of parental partnership marginalize parents. Parents, and particularly working-class parents, are seen as part of the problem, part of the 'odds' to be struggled against. The fragility and one-sided nature of the partnership is illustrated in the debate about home-school contracts which, to a large degree, have become a way of imposing discipline, rather than creating a partnership for learning (Vincent and Tomlinson, 1997). Clearly, there is much to be gained from involving parents in a close relationship with schools. Michael Barber has argued that parents should be compelled to attend meetings every six months at that child's school (Barber, 1996). Whether compelling, rather than welcoming, parents to visit the school will improve the relationship is debatable.

In some schools, parents are tolerated. In many they are welcomed, but as helpers and fund-raisers, rather than as co-educators. Schools make a range of assumptions when they approach the issue of parental involvement: about control; about the nature of parenting; about the support which parents can give to school; and about the parent as co-educator. Parental involvement as a strategy for controlling the behaviour of pupils is focused on ensuring that parents take responsibility for the behaviour of their children. The school sets out its expectations and, where possible, exerts leverage to ensure that parents and children comply.

> Parents were once kept out of school so as to allow professionals un-interrupted control: parents are now being encouraged to get involved and come into schools so that they can understand why the professional exercises control in the manner he/she does. (Cowburn, 1986, p. 18, quoted in Vincent and Tomlinson, 1997, p. 366)

Parental involvement has also been seen as a way of gaining support for specific school activities or objectives, and this has been a popular way of bringing parents into the life of the school, particularly in primary schools. It has practical advantages for schools and can also serve to reassure parents that all is well within the school. There is also another model, or set of assumptions, about parental involvement and this revolves around the idea of the parent as co-educator, responsible for the larger part of a child's life and education.

Whether these models are mutually exclusive depends on the starting point. If schools begin with the notion of parents as co-educators, as expressed in the Danish Folkeskole Act, then the other models can be accommodated. Parents can also be helpers, parents should take responsibility for their child's behaviour. Some parents do need support. If schools start by assuming that parents are co-educators, then they will work to find ways of including parents in having a say in shaping the school's priorities, and in setting the standards of behaviour expected of children — and parents and teachers. If schools start from the assumption that parents and pupils need to be controlled, then they will find that they are always having to look for new and tougher sanctions.

Notes

1   In December 1967, *The Observer* newspaper invited secondary school children to enter a competition. They were to describe 'The School that I'd Like'. The published selection of those entries remains a classic — full of passion, insights and critical reflections on the education system (Blishen, 1969).

2   In July 1997, I attended a conference hosted by the Rockefeller Foundation which focused on teachers and professionalism. In this section I have drawn on that conference and would like to thank the following for their contributions to my thinking: Deborah Loewenberg Ball, Miriam Ben-Peretz, Alain Bouvier, David Cohen, Linda Darling-Hammond, Margaret Garigan, Andy Hargreaves, Gaby Hostens, Jamie Beck Jensen, Philip Kearney, Magdalene Lampert, Sverker Lindblad, Judith Warren Little, Milbrey McLaughlin, Stephen Porch, Ellalinda Rustique-Forrester, Ted Sanders, Nobuo Ken Shimahara, Lee Shulman, Amy Tsui, Marla Ucelli, Johan Vonk and John Walshe.

3   The US has faced teacher shortages in central city and rural areas. Disparities in salaries and working conditions, and tendencies for state governments to lower entry requirements to solve the shortages, have meant that 'a growing number of poor children and children of color are being taught by teachers who are sorely prepared for the task they face' (Darling-Hammond and Cobb, 1996, p. 16).

4   Margaret Littlewood argues that the implicit assumption behind this notion of a 'narrow life' was that 'teaching attracted emotionally immature individuals, who preferred the sheltering body of the school to facing the demands of adult adjustment in the outside world'. She suggests that what constituted experience and maturity was gender specific. For men, it was experience in employment, for women it was the maturity which came from marriage and motherhood — the 'wise married women'. She goes on to argue that 'while the report implied rather than stated that women who were not married were unsuitable to be trained as teachers, others

were not as reticent. John Newsom in his book *The Education of Girls* (Newsom, 1948; p. 149) argued that single women teachers suffered from emotional problems arising from sexual repression or homosexuality. Married women teachers were also seen as inadequate if they were unhappily married' (Littlewood, 1989, pp. 182–3).

5   In thinking about professional development opportunities for teachers, American writers Deborah Loewenberg Ball and David Cohen counsel against the typical 'quick fix' model which is like 'yo-yo' dieting for most teachers, providing them with a few novel ideas but ultimately making little difference. They argue that teachers need to know about their subject matter, about children, about differences, about learning and about pedagogy. Through their professional development they need to learn about inquiry: how to investigate what students are doing and thinking, how to challenge their own thinking, and how to operate experimentally in response to students and situations (Ball and Cohen, 1996).

6   On the downside, initial teacher preparation in Japan is limited.

7   Writing in 1980, Miriam David saw this shift in the following terms:

> . . . the State has seen the existing education system as one of the major causes of economic crisis. Thus, reforms of the education system have been manifold: most of them have involved modifications to the involvement of both parents and teachers to schooling. Parents' responsibilities have been crucially redefined. In fact, parents have been offered a semblance of greater rights over their children's education, on the premise that this would encourage them to press for improvements in educational standards and hence in the conditions for the reproduction of capital. (David, 1980, p. 245)

8   There is evidence to suggest that pupils themselves play a significant part in the process of selecting a secondary school (Carroll and Walford, 1997). A study carried out in the early 1990s found that in two-fifths of the cases studied, choice of secondary schools was reported as having been a joint activity between parents and pupils. In just under a further two-fifths, pupils were reported to have made the choice themselves. There was also evidence to suggest that parents from higher socio-economic groups were less influenced by their child's preferences than parents from lower socio-economic groups (West, Varlaam and Scott, 1991).

9   In explaining this closure, Michael Barber, head of the Government's Standards and Effectiveness Unit argued that 1995 would be regarded by historians as the year in which a 'seismic shift in the culture became apparent'. From the mid-nineteenth century to the 1990s, a substantial failure rate amongst schools, teachers and pupils had been tolerated, he argued, however, '. . . 1995 is the year that failure at the rate we have known and accepted in the past became unacceptable' (Barber, 1995).

Chapter 10

Whose School is it Anyway? It's Ours

> Schools usually have one thing in common — they are institutions of today run on the principles of yesterday. 15-year-old girl (quoted in Blishen, 1969, Introduction)

Since Ancient Greek and Roman times the State has laid claim to control of teachers. Both Plato and Aristotle argued that the State should have a direct involvement in education. In Aristotle's view education was about citizenship and about developing the emotional side of human nature (Smith, 1946). Education was an enterprise in which the State needed to take a lead:

> No one will doubt that the legislator should direct his attention above all to the education of youth . . . The citizen should be moulded to suit the form of government in which he lives. (Aristotle, from *Politics*, quoted in Smith, 1946, p. 31)

In the eighteenth century, Rousseau argued for a degree of state control of education as a way of protecting the liberty of individuals. In the nineteenth century, John Stuart Mill said that the state should not control education but compel parents to do their duty in respect of their children. If necessary, the State should provide them with assistance in that task.

How far state control should extend has been an issue of debate and dispute — and periodic compromises — over nearly two centuries in Britain. There are issues about the relationship between the state and individuals; the state and parents; the state and the churches; the state and teachers; the state and local communities. The 1870 Forster Education Act signified that the state would take some responsibility for the well-being of children and that this would sometimes override the wishes of parents. The 1944 Act signalled a compromise between state, church, local government and teachers. Over recent decades, the state has held the ring in structuring the relationships between different groups: between teachers and governors, schools and parents, local authorities and schools, churches and schools.

Writing in the early 1940s, W.O. Lester Smith argued that the relationship between the state and society needed to be kept under careful scrutiny:

> There will (always) be subtle attempts at encroachment, imperceptible erosions and moves like the enclosure tactics which ate our common ground. (ibid. p. 198)

His analysis reminds us that the post-war consensus on education was based on a deeply held pre-war consensus about the danger of undue state control. In 1938, the Spens Report on secondary education saw the issue in the following terms:

> ... Observing, as one cannot now fail to do, how completely and exclusively the state may occupy that field (i.e. education) — turning the schools and the teachers into mere instruments of its policies, vehicles for the dissemination of the ideas it approves, and means for excluding from the minds of the young all ideas of which it disapproves — then we feel bound to assert our faith in the English compromise between state regulation and freedom of teaching, and to express the hope that circumstances will never arise to endanger its continuance. For where the schools lose their freedom, the freedom of the individual citizen is in peril. (The Spens Report,1938, Consultative Committee Report on Secondary Education, quoted in Smith, 1946, p. 8)

Exploring the question 'Whose School is it Anyway?' brings us face to face with the issue of state control: how far should state control and intervention extend, and how far should other groups have their say in school governance?

The last two decades have witnessed increasing state regulation over many aspects of education — curriculum, standards (for pupils and teachers) and, most recently, pedagogy. The control of education has moved, it has been argued, from a position of 'licensed autonomy' to one of 'regulated autonomy' (Dale, 1989, pp. 30–2). What children are to be taught, who is to teach it, and how, have become the business of government. Politicians have become increasingly preoccupied by league tables: school league tables, local authority league tables and national league tables, and there is a continuing drift towards the imposition of even greater government regulation in a belief that this will improve teaching and learning. The extreme cases — such as Tyndale — are used as evidence to remind us why this should be the case.

There is of course a balance to be struck between autonomy and control. In Chapter 1, I quoted a newspaper headline which followed the launch of the Government White Paper in 1997 — 'Government to Have its Hand in Every School' (Independent, 1997a). Whether this is to be a helping hand, or an iron hand (with or without the velvet glove) as yet remains unclear. It is always difficult for government to relinquish control, yet too much control will stifle creativity and innovation. What is needed now is a new compromise between state regulation and freedom of teaching. The government needs to set a vision, establish boundaries and expectations, and then stand back to enable others to ensure that the vision is achieved. Such an approach characterizes effective leadership at levels in the education system. Accountability needs increasingly to be expressed locally — through local authorities and school governing bodies, and within schools themselves, through the nature of their relationship with pupils and parents.

Once we have established higher entry standards for teachers, extended periods of probation and more stringent standards at every level of the profession, then we must learn to trust our teachers. Teachers can no longer be considered to be part of the problem and need to be seen as a crucial part of the answer. Entrusting teachers is not a foolish aspiration but a way of creating a robust model of teaching as a profession in which there is a degree of self-regulation and peer review, set against a framework of national standards, external validation and strong accountability. We will need to establish a contract of mutual expectations — What can society reasonably expect from teachers and, in return, what can teachers reasonably expect from society?

The stage at which government needs to intervene is in setting a framework which challenges fragmentation and exclusion, and which seeks to develop a more coherent and equitable education system. There is an urgent need to examine the contradictions in our current system and in our prevailing beliefs about education. Fragmentation, polarization and competition — all part of the 'Thatcher' legacy — sit uneasily within any conception of society in which aspirations, values and goals are shared, and in which diversity is recognized and valued.

There is an urgent need to meet the challenges of the disaffected. If our notion of society goes beyond the assertion of individual rights, policy-makers will need to reduce segregated structures in the educational system and create an inclusive system through the extension of comprehensive education, and the development of opportunities for greater integration of children with special needs. Schools will need to make provision for cultural diversity, reduce school failure and develop activities which are inclusive, rather than exclusive. Teachers will need to recognize diversity and identify and stimulate the strengths of students. Policy-makers, schools and teachers will need to accommodate the desire of young people to take control of their lives and their environment, and to develop a vision of the future which includes themselves.

There is, of course, no simple answer to the question 'Whose School is it Anyway?' But as part of the new dispensation, we need to give those closest to the school — those with most at stake — the biggest say, if the schools of today are to match the needs of tomorrow.

List of Interviewees

Robin Auld: Led the 'Auld' Inquiry (Now the The Rt Hon Lord Justice Auld, and Senior Presiding Judge for England and Wales).

Margaret Beckett: (nee Jackson): Junior Education Minister in 1976. Appointed as President of the Board of Trade and Industry in 1977.

Rhodes Boyson: Ex-Member of Parliament and Junior Education Minister, author of one of the 'Black Papers' (the Rt.Hon. Dr. Sir Rhodes Boyson).

Sheila Browne: Chief Inspector of Schools in 1976.

Tessa Blackstone: Member of the Central Policy Review Staff during the Callaghan administration and responsible for some of the policy developments post-Ruskin. As Baroness Blackstone appointed as Minister of State for Higher Education in 1997.

James Callaghan: Ex-Prime Minister (The Rt Hon Lord Callaghan of Cardiff).

Bernard Donoughue: Head of the Number 10 Policy Unit. Drafted 'Ruskin' speech along with Elizabeth Arnott (Now member of the House of Lords).

Elizabeth Hartley-Brewer: (nee Arnott): Member of the Number 10 Policy Unit who worked on the Ruskin speech with Bernard Donoughue.

Roy Hattersley: Member of the Callaghan Cabinet in 1976. Appointed to the House of Lords in 1997.

Fred Jarvis: Ex-General Secretary of the National Union of Teachers.

Maurice Kogan: Secretary to the Plowden Committee and Islington Green School Governor in 1976, (Professor at Brunel University).

David Lipsey: Policy Adviser to Tony Crosland in 1976 and in 1977 and member of the Number 10 Policy Unit (Political Editor of the *Economist*).

Margaret Maden: Headteacher of Islington Green School in 1976 (Professor at Keele University).

Peter Newsam: Took over as Administrative Leader of the ILEA in the wake of Tyndale and later became Sir Peter Newsam and the Director of the Institute of Education, University of London.

Anne Page: Ex-Islington Councillor and Member of the the ILEA (Director of the London Research Centre).

Chris Price: Ex-Member of Parliament and PPS to Fred Mulley, 1975–76.

Stephen Sedley: Barrister at the 'Auld' Inquiry representing Terry Ellis and colleagues (Lord Justice Sedley, QC).

References

ALBROW, M. (1994) 'Globalisation: Myths and realities'. Professorial Inaugural Lecture, London: The Roehampton Institute.

ALLEN, F. (1995) 'The politicisation of school governors', *Management in Education*, **9**, 3, June.

ALSALAM, N. and CONLEY, R. (1995) 'The rate of return to education: A proposal for a new indicator', in *Education and Employment*, Paris: Organisation for Economic Cooperation and Development.

ARCHER, M. (1979) *Social Origins of Educational Systems*, London: Sage Publications.

ARNOTT, M., BULLOCK, A. and THOMAS, H. (1992) 'Consequences of local management: An assessment by headteachers'. Paper presented at the Education Reform Act, Research Network, University of Warwick, March.

AULD, R. (1976) *William Tyndale, Junior and Infants Schools Public Inquiry*, A Report to the Inner London Education Authority by Robin Auld, QC, London: Inner London Education Authority.

BADDELEY, S. (1992) 'Integrity in a political environment'. Paper to the Canadian Association of School Administrators, Perspectives on Leadership.

BADDELEY, S. and JAMES, K. (1987) 'Owl, fox, donkey, or sheep: Political skills for managers', *Management Education and Development*, **18**, 1.

BALL, S. (1987) *The Micro-politics of the School*, London: Methuen.

BALL, S., BOWE, R. and GERWITZ, S. (1992) 'Circuits of schooling: A sociological exploration of parental choice of school in social class contexts', Swindon: Economic and Social Research Council.

BALL, D.L. and COHEN, D.K. (1995) 'Developing practice, developing practitioners: Toward a practice-based theory of professional education'. Paper prepared for the National Commission on Teaching and America's Future.

BARBER, M. (1995) 'The school that had to die', *Times Educational Supplement*, 17 November.

BARBER, M. (1996) *The Learning Game: Arguments for an Education Revolution*, London: Gollancz.

BARTLETT, W. (1994) 'Spoilt for choice', ESRC, Research Briefing Note no 9, *British Education Research Association, Research Intelligence*, **50**, Mid-summer.

BENN, C. and CHITTY, C. (1996) *Is Comprehensive Education Alive and Well, or Struggling to Survive?* London: David Fulton Publishers.

BENN, T. (1989) *Against The Tide, Diaries 1973–76*, London: Hutchinson.

BLACKSTONE, T. and PLOWDEN, W. (1990) *Inside the Think Tank: Advising the Cabinet 1971–83*, London: Mandarin.

BLISHEN, E. (1969) *The School That I'd Like*, London: Penguin Books in collaboration with 'The Observer'.

BOTTERY, M. and WRIGHT, N. (1997) 'Impoverishing a sense of professionalism: Who's to blame?' *Educational Management and Administration*, **25**, 1, Jan., pp. 7–24.

BOYD, W.L., CROWSON, R.L. and VAN GEEL, T. (1994) 'Rational choice theory and the politics of education: promise and limitations', *Politics of Education Association Yearbook, 1994*, pp. 127–45.

BRITISH BROADCASTING CORPORATION (1976) Radio Four, The World This Week End, 17 October.

BRITISH BROADCASTING CORPORATION (1989), *Public Affairs,* Programme 4, 'William Tyndale — School, or Scandal?' David Wheeler, 3 May, 7.20 pm.

BUSHER, H. and SARAN, R. (1994) 'Towards a model of school leadership', *Educational Management and Administration*, **22**, 1, pp. 5–13.

BUXTON, R. (1973) 'Comprehensive education: Central government, local authorities and the law', in FOWLER, G., MORRIS, V. and OZGA, J. (eds) *Decision Making in British Education*, London: Heinemann Books.

CALLAGHAN, J. (1976) 'Towards a national debate', (Text of the speech by the Prime Minister James Callaghan at a foundation-laying ceremony at Ruskin College, Oxford, on 18th October) *Education*, **148**, 17, pp. 334–5, 22 October.

CALLAGHAN, J. (1987) *James Callaghan: Time and Change*, Glasgow: William Collins Sons and Co. Ltd.

CALLAGHAN, J. (1992) 'The education debate', in WILLIAMS, M., DAUGHERTY, R. and BANKS, F. (eds) *Continuing the Education Debate*, London: Cassell.

CARROLL, S. and WALFORD, G. (1997) 'The child's voice in choice', *Educational Management and Administration*, **25**, 2, April, pp. 169–80.

CASTLE, B. (1993) *Fighting All the Way*, London: MacMillan.

CATHOLIC EDUCATION SERVICE (1997) *A Struggle for Excellence — Catholic Secondary Schools in Urban Poverty Areas*, London: CES.

CENTRE FOR POLICY STUDIES (1991) *End Egalitarian Delusion*, London: Centre for Policy Studies.

CPAG (1997) *Britain Divided*, London: Child Poverty Action Group.

CHUBB, J. and MOE, T. (1990) *A Lesson in School Reform for Great Britain*, Washington DC: Brookings Institute.

CLARKE, K. (1991) Speech to the Conservative Local Government Conference, 3 March.

COLEMAN, P., COLLINGE, J. and TABIN, Y. (1996) 'Learning together: The student/parent/teacher triad', *School Effectiveness and School Improvement*, **7**, 4, pp. 361–82.

COLEMAN, P. and LaROQUE, L. (1990) *Struggling to be Good Enough: Administrative Practices and School District Ethos*, London: Falmer Press.

References

COLEMAN, P. and RILEY, K.A. (1995) 'Accentuate the positive', *Education*, 14 July, pp. 11 and 18.

CONNAUGTON, S. (1977) *Sir is Winning*, A play performed at the Cottesloe National Theatre, London.

CORDINGLEY, P. and KOGAN, M. (1993) *In Support of Education*, London: Jessica Kingsley Publishers.

COUNCIL OF CHIEF STATE SCHOOL OFFICERS (1996) *Interstate School Leaders Licensure Consortium: Standards for School Leaders*, Washington, DC: CCSSO.

COWBURN, W. (1986) *Class, Ideology and Community Education*, London: Croom Helm.

Cox, C.B. and BOYSON, R. (1977) 'Black Paper 1977', *Critical Quarterly Society*.

Cox, C.B. and DYSON, A.E. (1971) *The Black Papers in Education*, Davis-Poynter.

CROSLAND, A. (1956) *The Future of Socialism*, London: Jonathon Cape Ltd.

CROSLAND, S. (1982) *Tony Crosland*, London: Jonathon Cape Ltd.

DAILY EXPRESS (1975a) 'Another term of trial for the class of '75', James Davies, 25 September, p. 10.

DAILY EXPRESS (1975b) 'Teachers' pawn', James Davies and John Burns, 25 September, p. 1.

DAILY EXPRESS (1997) 'Schools blitz as Blunkett goes back to basics', Patrick O'Flynn, p. 4.

DAILY MAIL (1975) 'Head who thought writing was obsolete', 29 October.

DAILY MAIL (1997a) 'Blunkett's great classroom gamble', Leo McKinstry, pp. 14–5, 8 July.

DAILY MAIL (1997b) 'Labour bans the s-word', Tony Halpin, 8 July, p. 1.

DAILY TELEGRAPH (1975) 'Parents boycott "school of shame" as teachers go back', Bruce Louden, 17 October, p. 6.

DAILY TELEGRAPH (1976) 'Managers, ILEA and staff all blamed for Tyndale "Chaos"', John Izbicki.

DAILY TELEGRAPH (1997a) 'Labour targets teachers in drive to improve standards, John Clare, 8 July.

DAILY TELEGRAPH (1997b) 'Blunkett's first test', Editorial, 8 July, p. 21.

DALE, R. (1989) *The State and Education Policy*, Milton Keynes: Open University Press.

DARLING-HAMMOND, L. and COBB, V.L. (1996) 'The changing context of teacher education', in MURRAY, F.B. (ed) *The Teacher Educator's Handbook: Building a Knowledge Base for the Preparation of Teachers*, San Francisco: Jossey-Bass.

DAVID, M.E. (1980) *The State, The Family and Education*, London: Routledge and Kegan Paul.

DAVIES, L. (1990) *Equality and Efficiency? School Management in the International Context*, London: Falmer Press.

DAVIN, A. (1996) *Growing Up Poor, Home School and Street Life in London 1870–1914*, London: Rivers Oram Press.

DAWSON, H. and RILEY, K.A. (1997) 'Lessons from failure', *Local Government Management*, **1**, 21, pp. 28–9.

144

DEEM, R. (1990) 'The reform of school governing bodies: The power of the consumer over the producer?' in FLUDE, M. and HAMMER, M. (eds) *The Education Reform Act 1988: Its Origins and Implications*, London: Falmer Press.

DEEM, R. (1993) 'Educational reform and school governing bodies in England 1986–92: Old dogs, new tricks or new dogs, new tricks?', in PREEDY, M. (ed) *Managing the Effective School*, London: Paul Chapman.

DES (1987) *Report by HM Inspectorate on Education in the outer London Borough of Brent*, Middlesex: Department of Education and Science.

DfEE (1997) *Framework for the Organisation of Schools: Technical Consultation Paper*, London: Department for Education and Employment, August.

DONOUGHUE, B. (1987) *Prime Minister: The Conduct of Policy under Harold Wilson and James Callaghan*, London: Jonathon Cape.

DUGUET, P. (1995) *Redefining the Place to Learn*, Paris: Organisation for Economic Cooperation and Development.

EARLEY, P. (1994) *School Governing Bodies — Making Progress?* Slough: National Foundation for Educational Research.

EARLEY, P., FIDLER, B. and OUSTON, J. (1996) 'Governing bodies, external inspections and "failing" schools'. Paper presented to the European Conference on Educational Research, University of Seville, September.

ECONOMIST (1997) 'Education white paper — lessons learnt', 12 July, p. 32.

(EDUCATION) WHITE PAPER (1996) London: HMSO.

ELLIS, T., McWHIRTER, J., McCOLGAN, D. and HADDOW, B. (1976) *William Tyndale — The Teachers' Story*, London: Writers and Readers Publishing Cooperative.

ELMORE, R.F. (1993) 'School centralization: Who gains? Who loses?' in HANNAWAY, J. and CARNOY, M. (eds) *Decentralization and School Improvement*, San Francisco: Jossey-Bass, pp. 35–54.

ELMORE, R.F. and FULLER, B. (1996) 'Empirical research on educational choice: What are the implications for policy-makers?' in FULLER, B. and ELMORE, R.F. with ORFIELD, G. (eds) *Who Chooses? Who Loses? Culture, Institutions and the Unequal Effects of School Choice*, New York: Teachers College Press.

EVENING NEWS (1975) 'Trotskyist teachers' warning to parents', 28 October.

EVENING STANDARD (1976) 'The classroom despots', Mary MacPherson, 18 July.

EVENING STANDARD (1997) 'Labour turns its back on years of "trendy teaching"', Dorothy Lepkowska, 7 July, p. 5.

FINANCIAL TIMES (1975) 'A radical experiment for our schools', 21 October.

FINANCIAL TIMES (1997a) 'Lessons from the old school', Simon Targett, 8 July.

FINANCIAL TIMES (1997b) 'New council to raise standing of teachers', Simon Targett, 25 July.

FINN, D., GRANT, N. and JOHNSON, R. (1977) 'Social democracy, education and the crisis', *Working Papers in Cultural Studies*, **10**, University of Birmingham: Centre for Contemporary Cultural Studies.

FITZ, J., HALPIN, D. and POWERS, S. (1993) *Grant-maintained Schools: Education in the Market Place*, London: Kogan Page.

FLOUD, J. (1961) 'Reserves of ability', *Forum*, **3**, 2, pp. 66–8.

FULLER, B. and ELMORE, R.F. with ORFIELD, G. (1996) *Who Chooses? Who Loses? Culture, Institutions and the Unequal Effects of School Choice*, New York: Teachers College Press.

GARDINER, G. (1975) *Margaret Thatcher: From Childhood to Leadership*, London: Kimber.

GOLDRING, E.B. (1994) 'The efficacy of public choice models in education: The case of Israel'. Paper to International Conference for School Effectiveness and Improvement, Melbourne.

GOLDRING, E.B., HAWLEY, W., SUFFOLD, R. and SMREKAR, C. (1994) 'The case for school choice; The promise of equity for students, families and schools'. Paper to International Conference for School Effectiveness and Improvement, Melbourne.

GRACE, G. (1995) *School Leadership: Beyond Educational Management*, London: Falmer Press.

GRAY, J. and WILCOX, B. (1994) 'Performance indicators: Flourish or perish?', in RILEY, K.A. and NUTTALL, D.L. (eds) *Measuring Quality, Education Indicators United Kingdom and International Perspectives*, London: Falmer Press.

GUARDIAN (1975a) 'Who can mediate in the class war?' 22 October.

GUARDIAN (1975b) 'Tyndale Seven complain of vicious campaign', 29 October.

GUARDIAN (1976) 'Tyndale school bosses resign', 21 July.

GUARDIAN (1997a) 24 June, p. 3.

GUARDIAN (1997b) '"Ambitious" plan excites teachers', John Carvel and Donald MacLeod, 8 July, p. 3.

HANSARD (1944) House of Commons Debate, 19 January, vol 396, col 209, London: HMSO.

HANSARD (1975) House of Commons Debate, 5 November (570–82), London: HMSO.

HANSARD (1976) House of Commons Debate, 19 October, London: HMSO.

HANSARD (1987) 'Order for the Second Reading of the Education Reform Bill', 1 December, London: HMSO.

HANSARD (1997a) 'School standards', 7 July, 613, London: HMSO.

HANSARD (1997b) 'Schools (White Paper)', 17 July, 593–94, London: HMSO.

HANUSHEK, E.A. WITH MEMBERS OF THE ECONOMICS OF EDUCATIONAL REFORM PANEL (1994) *Making Schools Work, Improving Performance and Controlling Costs*, Washington: The Brookings Institute.

HARGREAVES, A. (1991) 'Contrived collegiality: The micro politics of teacher collaboration', in BLASE, J. (ed.) *The Politics of Life in Schools: Power Conflict and Cooperation*, London: Sage.

HARGREAVES, A. (1997) 'Feeling like a teacher: The emotions of teaching and educational change', Paper submitted to *Phi Delta Kappan*.

HARGREAVES, D. (1995) 'School culture', *School Effectiveness and Improvement*, **6**, 1, March, pp. 23–45.

HATTERSLEY, R. (1997) 'Comparisons are otiose', *Times Educational Supplement*, White Paper Reactions, 15 August, p. 13.

HAYEK, F.A. (1991) *The Road to Serfdom*, London: Routledge.

HEALEY, D. (1989) *The Time of My Life*, London: Penguin.

HILL, S.M. and RAGLAND, J.C. (1995) *Women as Educational Leaders*, California: Corwen Press.

HOPKINS, D. (1992) 'Changing school culture through development planning', in RIDDELL, S. and BROWN, S. (eds) *School Effectiveness Research*, Edinburgh: HMSO.

HUBERMAN, M. (1993) 'The model of the independent artisans's professional relations', in LITTLE, J.W. and MC LAUGHLIN, M.W. (eds) *Teachers Work*, New York and London: Teachers' College Press.

INDEPENDENT (1991) 'A charter for schools', 5 June.

INDEPENDENT (1997a) 'Government to have its hand in every school', Lucy Ward, p. 8.

INDEPENDENT (1997b) 'Will Labour's plans pass the test?', Judith Judd, p. 16.

ITN (1976) *News at Ten*, 18 October.

KNIGHT, C. (1990) *The Making of Tory Education Policy in Post-war Britain: 1950–86*, London: Falmer Press.

KOGAN, M. (1971) *The Politics of Education*, London: Penguin.

KOGAN, M. (1978) *The Politics of Educational Change*, London: Fontana.

KOGAN, M. (1986) *Education Accountability: An Analytical Overview*, London: Hutchinson.

KOVACS, K. (1997) 'Combating failure', in RILEY, K.A. (ed) *International Issues in Education: Trends and Challenges*, London: Local Government Management Board.

KRUCHOV, C., MACBEATH, J. and RILEY, K.A. (1996) *Images of Leadership*, Scotland: University of Strathclyde.

LAMBETH (1987) *Whose Child? Report of the Public Inquiry into the Death of Tyra Henry*, chaired by Stephen Sedley, London Borough of Lambeth.

LASSWELL, H.D. (1936) *Politics: Who Gets What, When, How*, New York: McGraw-Hill.

LEAVIS, F.R. and THOMPSON, D. (1934) *Culture and Environment*, London: Chatto and Windus.

LEITHWOOD, K., BEGLEY, P.T. and COUSINS, J.B. (1994) *Developing Expert Leadership for Future Schools*, London: Falmer Press.

LEITHWOOD, K.A., LEONARD, L. and SHARRATT, T. (1997) 'Conditions fostering organisational learning in schools'. Paper presented to the International Congress for School Effectiveness and Improvement, Memphis, USA.

LEITHWOOD, K.A. and MONTGOMERY, D.J. (1982) 'The role of the elementary school principal in program improvement', *Review of Educational Research*, **52**, 3, pp. 309–39.

LEITHWOOD, K.A., STEINBACH, R. and BEGLEY, P.T. (1991) 'The nature and contribution of socialization experiences to becoming a principal in Canada'. Paper to the International Congress on School Effectiveness and Improvement, Cardiff.

LINKLATER, A. (1980) *An Unhusbanded Life: Charlotte Despard*, London: Hutchinson.

LITTLEWOOD, M. (1989) 'The "wise married woman" and the teacher unions', in DE LYON, H. and MIGNIUOLO, F.W. (eds) *Women Teachers, Issues and Experiences*, Milton Keynes: Open University Press.

LIVINGSTONE, K. (1976) 'How cuts hit William Tyndale'. Letter to the Hammersmith and Highgate newspaper, 6 August.

LOUIS, K.S., KRUSE, S.D. and ASSOCIATES (1995) *Professionalism and Community*, California: Corwin Press.

LUKES, S. (1974) Power, A Radical View, British Sociological Association, London and Basingstoke: Macmillan Press.

MACBEATH, J., MOOS, L. and RILEY, K.A. (1996) 'Leadership in a changing world', in LEITHWOOD, K.A., CHAPMAN, K., CORSON, C., HALLINGER, P. and HART, A. (eds) *International Handbook for Educational Leadership and Administration*, The Netherlands: Kluwer Academic Publishers.

MACBEATH, J. and RILEY, K.A. (1997) 'Issues in understanding leadership'. Working Paper to the International Conference for School Effectiveness and Improvement, Memphis.

MACNAIR (1944) *The Report of the Committee to Consider the Supply, Recruitment and Training of Teachers and Youth Workers*, London: HMSO.

MAHONY, P. (1995) 'School governance in England and Wales', *Working Paper, Effective Leadership in a Time of Change*, London: The Roehampton Institute.

MAHONY, P. and RILEY, K.A. (1995) 'Headteachers in the English LEAs: Initial analysis of some themes and issues', Conference Report Edinburgh, *Effective Leadership in a Time of Change*, London: The Roehampton Institute.

MANLEY-CASIMIR, M. (1991) 'Taking the road not taken: Reframing education administration for another day — a critique', in RIBBINS, P., GLATTER, R., SIMKINS, T. and WATSON, L. (eds) *Developing Education Leaders*, Harlow: Longman, in association with BEMAS.

MCKENZIE, P. (1997) 'The transition from school to work', in RILEY, K.A. (ed.) *International Issues in Education: Trends and Challenges*, London: Local Government Management Board.

MURPHY, J. (1994) 'Transformational change and the evolving role of the principal', in MURPHY, J. and LOUIS, K.S. (eds) *Reshaping the Principalship: Insights from Transformational Reform Efforts*, Thousand Oaks, CA: Corwin Press.

MURPHY, J. and LOUIS, K.S. (1994) *Reshaping the Principalship: Insights for Transformational Reform Efforts*, Thousand Oaks, CA: Corwin Press.

THE NATIONAL COMMISSION ON TEACHING AND AMERICA'S FUTURE (1996) *What Matters Most: Teaching for America's Future*, Washington, DC: US Department of Education.

NEWSAM, P. (1981) *The Inner London Education Authority, 1970–1980, Ten Years of Change*, London: ILEA.

NEWSAM, P. (1994) 'Last bastion against the mighty state', Governors Guide, *Times Educational Supplement*, 30 September.

NEWSOM, J. (1948) *The Education of Girls*, London: Faber.

OBSERVER (1976) 'The tragedy of William Tyndale', Colin Cross, 18 July.

OECD (1994) *Quality in Teaching*, Paris: Organisation for Economic Cooperation and Development.

OECD (1995a) Meeting of the Education Committee at Ministerial Level, Background Report, Chapter 2, 'Towards lifelong learning for all: aims barriers and strategies', Note by the Secretary-General, Paris: Organisation for Economic Cooperation and Development.

OECD (1995b) *Education at a Glance, OECD Indicators*, Paris: Organisation for Economic Cooperation and Development.

OECD (1996a) *Making Lifelong Learning a Reality for All*, Paris: Organisation for Economic Cooperation and Development.

OECD (1996b) *Education at a Glance, OECD Indicators*, Paris: Organisation for Economic Cooperation and Development.

OECD (1997) *Families and Schools*, Paris: Organisation for Economic Cooperation and Development.

PAGE, A. (1976) 'Statement to the Special Meeting of the ILEA Schools Sub-Committee', County Hall, July 21.

PEDLEY, R. (1963) *The Comprehensive School*, London: Penguin.

PEERS, R. (1963) *Fact and Possibility in English Education*, London: Routledge and Kegan Paul.

PHILLIPS, M. (1996) *All Must Have Prizes*, London: Little, Brown and Company.

PLOWDEN (1967) *The Plowden Report, Children and Their Primary Schools*, Report of the Central Advisory Council for Education (England): London, HMSO.

POLLITT, C., BIRCHALL, S. and PUTMAN, K. (1997) *Opting Out and the Experience of Self-Management in Education, Housing and Health Care*, ESRC Local Governance Programme, Working Paper 2, Economic and Social Research Council.

POSCH, P. (1996) 'Teachers and their professional development', OECD Project, *Teachers and Curriculum Reform in Basic Schooling*, Paris: Centre for Educational Research and Innovation, Organisation for Economic Co-operation and Development.

RAISON, T. (1990) *Tories and the Welfare State*, London: MacMillan.

RANSON, S. (1993) 'Reviewing education for democracy'. Paper presented at the Institute of Public Policy Research Seminar on Alternative Education Policies, London, March.

RANSON, S. and THOMAS, H. (1989) 'Education reform: Consumer democracy, or social democracy', in STEWART, J. and STOKER, G. (eds) *The Future of Local Government*, Basingstoke, Macmillan Education.

RIBBINS, P. (1989) 'Managing secondary schools after the act: Participation and partnership?', in LOWE, R. (ed.) *The Changing Secondary School*, London: Falmer Press.

RILEY, K.A. (1992) 'The changing framework and purpose of education authorities', Research Papers in Education Policy and Practice, **7**, 1, March, pp. 3–25.

References

RILEY, K.A. (1994a) *Managing Myths and Magic in Education*, Inaugural Lecture, London: The Roehampton Institute.

RILEY, K.A. (1994b) *Managing for Quality in an Uncertain Climate*, Luton: Local Government Management Board.

RILEY, K.A. (1994c) *Quality and Equality, Promoting Opportunities in School*, London: Cassell.

RILEY, K.A. (1997) 'Changes in local governance — collaboration through networks: A post-16 case study', *Education Management and Administration*, **25**, 2, April, pp. 155–68.

RILEY, K.A., JOHNSON, H. and ROWLES, D. (1995) *Managing for Quality in an Uncertain Climate, Report II*, Luton: Local Government Management Board.

RILEY, K.A. and ROWLES, D. (1997a) *From Intensive Care to Recovery: Schools Requiring Special Measures*, London: London Borough of Haringey.

RILEY, K.A. and ROWLES, D. (1997b) 'Inspection and school improvement in England and Wales: National contexts and local realities', in TOWNSEND, T. (ed.) *Restructuring, Quality and Effectiveness: Problems and Possibilities for Tomorrow's Schools*, London: Routledge.

RILEY, K.A. with ROWLES, D. (1997c) 'School governors: an experiment long in the making', in FIDLER, B., RUSSELL, S. and SIMKINS, T. (eds) *Choices for Self-managing Schools: Autonomy and Accountability*, London: Paul Chapman.

ROSENER, J.B. (1990) 'Ways women lead', *Harvard Business Review*, November/December.

RUBINSTEIN, D. and SIMON, B. (1973) *The Evolution of the Comprehensive School, 1928–1972*, London: Routledge and Kegan Paul.

RUBY, A. (1995) 'Reforming education'. Invited Lecture, The Roehampton Institute, London, November.

RUDDOCK, J. (1996) 'Students' voices: what can they tell us as partners in change?' Address to the 5th BEMAS Research Conference, Partners in Change: Shaping the Future, March, Cambridge.

SALLIS, J. (1988) 'Back to the future', *Times Educational Supplement*: The Governors' Guide, November.

SCHOOL BOARD OF LONDON MINUTES (1888) East Lane school, Southwark, 3 August, p. 1,374 in DAVIN, A. (1996) *Growing Up Poor, Home School and Street Life in London 1870–1914*, London: Rivers Oram Press.

SHARP, R. and GREEN, A. with LEWIS, J. (1975) *Education and Social Control: A study in Progressive Primary Education*, London: Routledge and Kegan Paul.

SHULMAN, L.S. (1987) 'Knowledge and teaching: Foundations of the new reform', *Harvard Educational Review*, **57**, 1, pp. 1–22, February.

SMITH, L.W.O. (1946) *To Whom Do Schools Belong? An Introduction to the Study of School Government*, 2nd Ed., Oxford: Basil Blackwell.

SMITH, S. (1997) 'Targeting and control in the finance of local services'. Paper to the ESRC Local Governance Programme Conference, Glasgow, April.

SMYLIE, M.A. (1992) 'Teacher participation in school decision making; Assessing willingness to participate', *Educational Evaluation and Policy Analysis*, **14**, 1, pp. 53–67.

SOCIALIST TEACHER (1977) 'Lessons of Tyndale', **3**, Autumn, pp. 8–11.

STOLL, L. and FINK, D. (1992) 'Effecting school change: The Halton approach', *School Effectiveness and Improvement*, **3**, pp. 19–41.

TALBERT, J.E. and MCLAUGHLIN, W. (1994) 'Teacher professionalism in local school contexts', *American Journal of Education*, **102**, pp. 123–53.

TEACHER TRAINING AGENCY (1997) *'National Standards for Headteachers'*, London TTA.

TIMES (1975a) 'Teachers refuse to let managers in to school for inspection', 2 July.

TIMES (1975b) 'Children from William Tyndale School "blacked"', Mark Jackson, 5 December.

TIMES (1976) Editorial, 19 October.

TIMES EDUCATIONAL SUPPLEMENT (1976a) July 23, p. 1.

TIMES EDUCATIONAL SUPPLEMENT (1976b) 'Great Debate opens with an anticlimax', 22 October, p. 1.

TIMES EDUCATIONAL SUPPLEMENT (1996a) September 6, pp. 4–6.

TIMES EDUCATIONAL SUPPLEMENT (1996b) September 6, p. 15.

TIMES EDUCATIONAL SUPPLEMENT (1997a) 'Home-school contact law to go', 15 August, p. 9.

TIMES EDUCATIONAL SUPPLEMENT (1997b) 1 August, p. 3.

TIMES HIGHER EDUCATION SUPPLEMENT (1997) 'Government in retreat after gap-year fiasco', August 15, p. 1.

TIMMINS, N. (1995) *The Five Giants: A Biography of the Welfare State*, London: Fontana Press.

TOMLINSON, J. (1993) *The Control of Education*, London: Cassell.

VERNON, P.E. (1957) *Secondary School Selection*, London: Methuen.

VINCENT, C. and TOMLINSON, S. (1997) 'Home-school relationships', *British Educational Research Journal*, **23**, 3, pp. 361–77.

WAINWRIGHT, H. (1994) *Arguments for a New Left: Answering the Free-market Right*, Oxford: Blackwell.

WALKER, D. (1974) 'A criticism of the "Free Choice" method of education based on total children's rights as at William Tyndale Junior School'.

WALSH, K. (1991) 'Rights, charters and contracts', in RILEY K.A. (ed.) *Education a Major Local Authority Service?* Working Papers from the Project, Luton: Local Government Management Board.

WAPSHOTT, N. and BROCK, G. (1983) *Thatcher*, London: MacDonald/Futura.

WEST, A., VARLAAM, A. and SCOTT, G. (1991) 'Choice of high schools: Pupils' perceptions', *Educational Research*, **33**, 3, pp. 205–15.

WHITE PAPER (1997) *Excellence in Schools*, London: HMSO.

WHITTY, G. (1997) 'Creating quasi-markes in education: A review of recent research on parental choice and school autonomy in three countries', *Review of Research in Education*, **22**, pp. 3–47, published by the American Educational Research Association.

References

WILBY, P. (1975) 'A lesson for the teachers, *New Statesman*, 5th December.

WILBY, P. (1997a) *New Statesman*, 11 July, pp. 13–14.

WILBY, P. (1997b) 'Local lessons', *New Statesman*, 25 July, p. 20.

WILLETTS, D. (1992) *Modern Conservatism*, Harmondsworth: Penguin.

WOODHEAD, C. (1997) 'Annual Lecture of the Chief Inspector of Schools', London: Royal Society of Arts.

WOODS, P. (1993) 'Responding to the consumer: Parental choice and school effectiveness', *School Effectiveness and School Improvement*, **4**, 3, pp. 205–29.

Index